# Unpacking for Greece

## Sally Jane Smith

Journeys in Pages

First published by Journeys in Pages, 2023

This book is a work of memoir, and therefore relies on the author's memories, opinions and ideas. While it is a recording of true events, some names have been changed, there are minor shifts or compressions in timeline, the dates of some social media posts have been brought forward a few days to match the incident described, and dialogue has been presented to the best of the author's recollection. The factual material in the book has been prepared with the author's best efforts, but it is not intended as an academic text and is of the nature of general comment only.

ISBN 978-0-6456257-0-7 (paperback)
ISBN 978-0-6456257-1-4 (e-book)

Cover design by Andrew Brown of Design for Writers
Internal design by Rebecca Brown of Design for Writers

The Lawrence Durrell quotation is reproduced with permission of Curtis Brown Group Ltd, London on behalf of The Estate of Lawrence Durrell. Copyright © Lawrence Durrell

A catalogue record for this book is available from the National Library of Australia

# CONTENTS

Map of Greece..........................................................*ix*

**Before: Trauma, Migration and Middlescence** ..... *1*

Chapter One • It Began in Sri Lanka ........................ *3*
Chapter Two • A New Life in Australia...................... *9*

**Craving Change: A Greek Adventure**................. *17*

Chapter Three • Arriving in Greece ........................*19*
Chapter Four • Athens to the Lake and Back..............*27*
Chapter Five • Icons of Athens .............................*41*
Chapter Six • Athens to Monemvasia ......................*55*
Chapter Seven • Basil, Books and Monemvasia's
    Byzantine Laneways....................................*69*
Chapter Eight • Monemvasia to Methana, via Sparta.....*81*
Chapter Nine • Methana Meditations ......................*93*
Chapter Ten • Methana to Meteora........................ *107*
Chapter Eleven • Meteora's World Heritage ............ *121*
Chapter Twelve • Monopatia and Moussaka in Meteora... *133*
Chapter Thirteen • Meteora to the Cauldron of Santorini... *147*
Chapter Fourteen • Santorini Sunset..................... *157*
Chapter Fifteen • Solo on Santorini ...................... *165*
Chapter Sixteen • Santorini to Rhodes ................... *175*
Chapter Seventeen • Rhodes Roamings................... *183*
Chapter Eighteen • Wrapping Up in Rhodes............. *193*

Chapter Nineteen • Heading Home: A Facebook Log... *207*

**After: Reflections** ............................................... *209*

Chapter Twenty • Looking Back............................ *211*

Epilogue • A Quest and a Cover ........................... *221*

**What Happened Next** ...................................... *227*

Book Two: Chapter One • Remembering Apartheid
        South Africa ............................................. *229*

Acknowledgements .......................................... *241*

# Map of Greece

A - Athens
B - Monemvasia
C - Sparta
D - Methana
E - Meteora
F - Santorini
G - Rhodes

# BEFORE: TRAUMA, MIGRATION AND MIDDLESCENCE

# CHAPTER ONE
## IT BEGAN IN SRI LANKA

THE SOUND WAS BRUTAL, a clap of thunder that split my world into the before and the after. What followed was surreal, impressions flickering like images in an old movie:

Silence, broken by children's cries.

A gradual awareness of fluid running down my neck.

Solving the riddle of whether – and how – to raise a hand to touch it.

An unhurried examination of the redness coating my fingertips and the intriguing thought, *It's blood*. And then, *It's my blood*.

The clump of fair hair, torn from someone's scalp, lying at my feet. I considered it with careful logic until I reasoned out from the colour that it must be mine.

A vague awareness that I couldn't see out of my left eye. I wondered if I'd lost my sight, not understanding that a curtain of blood was shrouding half my vision.

No pain at first, just a trance of stillness and the slow flow of time. My eyes fixed on those of a pregnant woman sitting across from me. Flecks of blood spotted her dress.

Uncountable minutes slipped by as I dipped in and out of reality, as detached from my surroundings as if they were a jumble of pieces from someone else's puzzle. Then the sudden agony of whiplash set in, wrenching me out of my daze. A stranger stood, beckoning, in the open doorway of the bus. I heaved myself out of my seat and stumbled towards him, only to lose consciousness. When I came round, two men were carrying me like a rag doll to a waiting vehicle, their arms hooked under my knees and shoulders.

The vehicle wasn't an ambulance. A third bus had halted, its passengers spilling out to gather the wounded from the two that had collided. As it jolted into motion, I heard words in English, spoken in a sweet singsong, over and over: 'Don't worry. Hospital. Don't worry.'

Then there were the hours awaiting surgery in a run-down district hospital, the long darkness of a fearful night, the indignities eclipsed by pain, and the relief when Aruna unexpectedly appeared at my bedside at half past six on the morning after the accident. We'd met only twice before, but Aruna had travelled for three hours over unlit, potholed jungle roads to reach me. It would be another eighteen hours before he could get me to Colombo and one of Sri

Lanka's finest medical institutions, then drive the long road back to his wife and young children in Kandy.

The sterile magnificence of Apollo Hospital was a sharp contrast to the primitive facilities in the district ward where nursing staff had dropped me, unable to sit without support, onto a cement bathroom floor and directed me to defecate. It had been a pointless command, as bowel movements were low on my body's list of priorities for weeks after the accident.

This new hospital immersed me in modernity and the acrid smell of disinfectant. Its atrium was nothing short of majestic, reaching up through multiple storeys. When they first wheeled my gurney under that soaring space, I watched the ceiling fall away beneath me with a vertiginous thrill as I glided over the abyss, my perspective deliciously skewed by morphine. As we moved from one corridor to another, our smooth passage through each doorway filled me with a haze of blissful surprise: I expected the wheels to collide with every lintel under which we travelled.

~ ~ ~

My story belongs in Greece, but it started in the front passenger seat of a battered old bus, a decade earlier and half a world away.

I'd landed in Sri Lanka the week before, eager for a solo adventure. Within days, I had thrilled to live music in Kandy, bottle-fed a rescued baby elephant and struggled up 5,200 chilly steps to summit Sri Pada before daybreak. There were the painted cave temples of Dambulla to explore, and an ascent between massive stone lion's paws to the highest point of the fortress rock of Sigiriya. I walked the clockwise circuit of a twelfth-century stupa in Polonnaruwa's pelting monsoon rain and marvelled at the colossal reclining Buddha carved into living rock at the Gal Vihara.

A train ticket, costing the rupee equivalent of one Australian dollar and change, took me on a slow, seventy-kilometre journey into the heart of Sri Lanka. My eyes feasted on the rolling green landscape – so different from the arid flatness of Abu Dhabi, where I worked as a teacher – and my ears danced to the drumming of a friendly jam session echoing the *clack-clack* of the train.

With no available seats, I took my turn sitting in an open doorway, my back resting against the steel plate of the carriage wall, and my left arm hooked around a metal bar. Those were the days when I trusted in the strength of that arm.

Despite the hours of standing and the rank smell from the toilet, that journey brought me real joy. There is a buzz of excitement in the electric rhythm of train travel, but there is also a comfort in riding the rails, a confidence that you'll arrive at your destination. Unlike a bus, which could veer off in any direction, there's little chance that a train will go off track. But my itinerary didn't follow the train lines, so most of my Sri Lankan travels were by road.

On 27 January 2006, a week into my Sri Lankan holiday, I was the only foreigner on the bus from Polonnaruwa to Anuradhaphura. The ticket-sellers' repetitive cries rolled in the air like a mantra as I paid seventy Aussie cents for the 101-kilometre journey to Sri Lanka's ancient Sinhalese capital. A fine rain was falling, a rare pleasure for a desert-dweller like me. As I sat in the crowded bus, munching my way through a packet of cashews, a rush of fulfilment swept through me.

*This*, I understood in an instant of clarity as the bus swerved through the reckless confusion of traffic, *is what my travels are all about*. Every step into day-to-day local life was an accomplishment. Deciphering a map, managing a purchase with exotic coinage or finding the right bus were important victories in each day's quest. Transient links – a shared kindness with a fellow passenger or a flashed smile in a moment of humour – were even more precious than the sense of connection that swelled in my breast when I wandered the world's heritage sites. Navigating through unknown landscapes, while grappling with an unfamiliar language, was the most wonderful adventure. And, when things didn't go according to plan, I'd laugh at myself and do my utmost to wring every ounce of enjoyment from the unexpected. *There aren't many travel experiences more rewarding than undertaking the practical task of getting from Point A to Point B, whether on foot or using public transport.*

It is a cruel irony that this realisation struck just minutes before we slammed, head-on, into another bus.

# CHAPTER TWO
# A NEW LIFE IN AUSTRALIA

I WAS A BROKEN BODY when I returned home to Abu Dhabi, accompanied by a repatriation nurse and my sister, Tassin, who had flown from Australia to help. I thought the ordeal was over, something to put behind me. But my recovery has been its own muddled jigsaw puzzle, each piece demanding all my energy until I could slot it into place:

The red welt of a scar, running halfway around my neck, that has faded with the years.

The chronic pain that has dwindled over a decade to little more than an uncomfortable stiffness in my shoulder. It sometimes creeps up the side of my neck, where the flesh tingles with a weird semi-numbness.

The neurological damage, diagnosed as an 'upper trunk pathology, particularly affecting the C5 nerve root', that has left me with a restricted range of movement in one arm, a sloping shoulder and some weakness on my left side. This is a minimal disability: a muttering nuisance, inaudible to others. Invisible, unless I am seeking serenity through a series of yoga poses, or beating my frustrations into the skin of a Taiko drum.

My lingering unease about being the first patient examined when we arrived at the district hospital in Polonnaruwa. Was it because my visible injuries were the most serious, as Tassin has assured me? Or was it because mine was the only foreign face on the bus?

The anger that simmered inside me at having survived. Doctors in both Colombo and Abu Dhabi warned me about this, or something similar. 'Depression,' they said. But it shocked me when it erupted. Its power left me raging at the walls of my flat, shuddering with furious sobs and ranting at fate for letting me live.

I remind myself that I was very lucky. But I have never recovered the person I was before one bus smashed into another. It's as if those jigsaw pieces were pressed into the wrong gaps, failing to replicate the picture on the box.

Five months after the accident, I finished up my teaching contract in the United Arab Emirates. I had a job offer in my South African hometown, but Tassin insisted I stop over in Australia first to recuperate. It turned out 'recuperation' meant three months of sweeping up kangaroo poo at Walkabout Park, the wildlife sanctuary she managed on the New South Wales Central Coast. To be fair, it was great physiotherapy. Mental therapy, too, now I come to think of it.

While in Australia, I tried to find out what had happened to my fellow passengers. The memory of blood-spattered fabric stretched taut over a pregnant belly haunted me. Most of my queries went unanswered, but the Acting Consul General of Sri Lanka responded. She'd contacted her country's tourist board in an attempt to learn more about the incident, but they were unable to uncover further details. All I'll ever know came from the doctor triaging patients in Polonnaruwa: one passenger had died in the crash itself.

The visit to Australia led me to move here a couple of years later to help my sister run her wildlife park. Adam, an Aussie firefighter, stopped by one morning to ask about our volunteer ranger program, and my planned two-year stay unfurled to eight years, and beyond. Back in Cape Town, a *Les Misérables*-style barricade lurked in my friend Megan's spare room, awaiting my return. Off-limits to her curious cats, it was a tangle of my grandmother's dining chairs and gate-leg table, my mother's bookcases, boxes labelled 'Kitchen' or 'Travel Pics' and bags of clothes that might never fit me again.

Meanwhile, the untamed travel that had been such an important part of my identity diminished. I made trips to South Africa to visit family and journeyed around Australia with Adam. After some persuasion – without even wondering why I needed persuading – I ventured to Europe to meet up with Megan and then Shauna, both lifelong friends, choosing destinations that felt easy and safe. There were two South

Pacific Ocean cruises with Tassin: the essence of relaxation, but not what I'd call *travel*. I never took those opportunities for granted, never stopped telling myself how privileged I was, but my ferocious appetite for taking on the world had vanished.

The closest I came to recapturing this wanderlust was on a trip Adam and I took through India with two yoga teachers we'd met at Prema Shanti, a serene retreat in far northern Queensland. Our group included nine yogis, a full-time Australian tour operator and a succession of Indian drivers and guides. Yet, even with such an entourage taking care of all the arrangements, I almost couldn't face the journey. The cacophonous chaos of India's traffic is infamous, and I foresaw the anxiety that would ripple through me each time we took to the road.

Like the echoing tones that Mara coaxed from her bronze singing bowl to rouse us from *shav asana*, India's ringing chords set off a resonance deep inside me. It murmured in the voices of Tibetan refugees – some in jeans, a few in saffron robes – as we huddled on the floor of a Himalayan school, and whistled in the breeze that blessed our rooftop yoga practice alongside the rushing River Ganges. It didn't quite reawaken my dormant hunger for solo travel, but I heard it stirring for the first time in years.

After our final yoga class, Mara asked each member of the group to share what the trip had meant to us. I surprised myself, and startled Adam, by breaking into a turmoil of gulping sobs. For me, it had been a two-week-long silent confrontation with fear.

Now, I was in my mid-forties. And we all know what that means. Not, I hasten to add, that this had anything to do with my relationship. Despite a niggling awareness that our partnership blocked an escape route I'd taken more than once before – migrating to a new country, shedding emotional baggage as I went – Adam and I were good together. This is not a *Shirley Valentine* story.

Life was pleasant, but mundane. I'd moved from Walkabout Park to a nearby town, where I worked in an office just three minutes' stroll from the modest flat I shared with Adam. Lunch-hour gym classes weren't much further away. As an introvert who shuts down early in the evenings, I seldom went out except for local drumming circles, book-club gatherings at our neighbourhood cocktail bar, or weekend walks with rescue animals from the community dog shelter. Occasionally, we took the train to Sydney to see a show or an art exhibition. I was more likely to head straight home after work – no lengthy commute for me – and sink into a hot bath with a book and a glass of wine before my colleagues had finished battling the traffic to reach their families.

Then a strange combination of stress and futility overtook my workplace. A restructure unravelled our close-knit business unit, splitting our five teams between three corporate departments. I marked time, trying to be useful wherever I could, while the organisation decided where to place me. It was a far cry from the career I'd loved.

I lost my last sense of purpose.

It helped a bit when I compared my life with that of my mother. Or, at least, as I had witnessed it from the self-centred viewpoint of a young daughter.

Hers seemed a narrow life, defined by her husband and six children, duty to her imperfect parents who had split up when she was little and packed her off to boarding school, and the Roman Catholic faith to which she'd converted in her twenties. Don't get me wrong: she lived this life to the fullest. I never heard my parents argue, not even once, and I believe they were content with their marriage and proud of the home they made for our family. But this homemaking came at a cost. She told me, one of the few times we talked about anything meaningful, that from the birth of her first baby until the last of my siblings left home, she had been childrearing for forty-two years. I had so many more opportunities than she ever had. My life had been much broader, if not as deep.

How arrogant, how insensitive it is to complain about the banality of an easy life of simple pleasures. But that's how it was. I was in my forties and having a midlife crisis. Actually, I couldn't even claim something quite so dramatic. It was more a middlescence, a time of restlessness, frustration, alienation.

'Middlescence' is a word I learned recently, but my computer's spellchecker failed to recognise it. Instead, it suggested the alternatives 'mindlessness' and 'indecency'. Was it indecent to feel so mindlessly discontented with such a comfortable life?

The only thing I could think of to resolve this middlescence, this indecent mindlessness, was to travel, alone, somewhere marvellous. Somewhere rich in heritage and enticing foods. Somewhere I'd have to come to grips with an unknown language. Somewhere I would need to find my way about by train and by boat and on foot…

… and by bus.

# CRAVING CHANGE: A GREEK ADVENTURE

# CHAPTER THREE
## ARRIVING IN GREECE

I T TOOK FOUR PLANES and forty-four hours of travel to reach my hotel in Athens.

A light glowed from the lobby, showing a mirror that reflected the words 'Art Gallery Hotel' spelled out in brass capitals. Below the reversed letters, a black-and-white tuxedo cat lay curled on a chair. When I tripped on the front step – unsuccessful in my attempt to juggle suitcase, fatigue and habitual clumsiness – he opened a grumpy eye, then rose and stretched. Untangling myself from my backpack and water bottle sling, I offered a hand in apology. He pressed his arched back against my palm with a rumbling purr. 'That's Arti,' said the receptionist. 'He likes you.' She sounded surprised.

Exhaustion had wound me so tight that there was no chance of dropping off to sleep anytime soon. I headed up the narrow spiral staircase to the fourth storey, where the breakfast-room-cum-reading-lounge became a terrace bar at eight o'clock each night. And I took with me something precious, something I had been saving for this moment.

~ ~ ~

When I was little, my mum went on a pilgrimage to Jerusalem and the Vatican with my grandmother and a group from their church. Already in her forties and the mother of three boys and three girls, aged from twenty-four down to just six, it was only the second time she had been overseas. She'd have considered herself fortunate. Many of her friends had never travelled out of the country at all.

The pilgrims' itinerary included an audience with the new pope, but this plan was spectacularly scuppered when John Paul I died two days before they flew out of South Africa. They were in Rome for the papal funeral, which they watched in their hotel's television lounge on a rainy Wednesday afternoon. They spent three nights in Greece on their way home, the adventure of a lifetime for my mother. All that mattered to me as a six-year-old, though, was that they returned bearing gifts. Among the parcels were matching 'Greek peasant blouses' for me and my seventeen-year-old sister, Tassin.

Tassin was allowed to wear hers off-the-shoulder. I was not. This was a dreadful disappointment and an early lesson in life not being fair.

I hadn't thought of Mum's mini odyssey in years. Maybe decades. Perhaps not since before her death as one millennium prepared to tick over to the next. And I'd never known she'd kept a travel journal, a tiny thing that almost fitted in the palm of my hand. When my sisters heard I'd be flying to Greece, Tassin went fossicking through long-neglected papers to find it. It was too late to influence my choice of six destinations across the Greek mainland and islands but, after she photographed each page for safekeeping, I stowed it in my hand luggage and brought it with me to Europe.

~ ~ ~

Nursing an ouzo at a table on the hotel's fourth-floor terrace, I opened the scuffed red cover of my mother's pocket diary for the first time and turned to the entries she wrote in October 1978.

*Date* Tues 17th *Place* Jerusalem Athens

Such a night! But back to the beginning. Packed. No breakfast. Off to mass at Gethsemane. English speaking Camel Zuzu... Footprint. Pater Noster Church – even Braille. To Jaffa gate. St. Anthony had this Note book for me at Holy Sepulchre... Dan picked us up and off to airport. Ticket not

21

signed so dragged off by Security. O.K. Bought ½
Jack brandy $1.75. 5 x tea $3.00! Got to Athens
½ hr late. Met by George and off to Damon
Hotel. All met at 7 + off to PLAKA by bus. To
Giovetsakia taverna + Belly dancer with Johnny
very disapproving…

*Whose footprint? And what's a Camel Zuzu?* Apart from
appreciating Mum's bewilderment at their tea costing
more than a round of brandy, the words meant little to
me. We'd struggled to communicate when she was alive,
so this shouldn't have been a surprise. I'd been hoping for
an instantaneous flare of connection, but there wasn't even
a spark.

After a frustrating half hour of poring over tiny pages
filled with cramped handwriting, I glanced up. And there
it was, a bright patch floating above the darkness that was
the hill of the Acropolis. The Parthenon! Despite its aura of
illumination, less than a kilometre away, I'd been oblivious
to one of the planet's most recognisable buildings – a sure
sign of fatigue. Getting up, I mopped spilt drops of ouzo
from my unassuming table with its world-famous view. It
was time for bed.

~ ~ ~

My body was reeling from the long series of flights – the price of travel on the cheap – but jet lag woke me early. Minutes after the breakfast room opened, I was tucking into a plain but filling meal which, surprisingly, included olives.

I didn't like olives. I found them quite nasty and would pick them off pizzas and out of salads. My sister Jenny, the matriarch of the family since our mum died, used to say they were an acquired taste, but I never saw the point of acquiring yet another high-calorie inclination. Besides, I didn't believe her. And despite my globetrotting past, I had a fixed idea of the range of foods suitable for breakfast, with cereals at one end of the continuum and scrambled eggs on toast at the other. But I was in Greece and the olives were staring back at me, so I took two and ate them in tiny nibbles with lots of bread and cheese to take the edge off their strong flavour.

The Parthenon was visible from my breakfast table, floating above Athens like a halo, but I had no feel for the layout of the city. I hadn't yet unpacked the guidebook information crammed into my mind from hours of study on the plane. Luckily, I had anticipated I'd be embarking on this first day with a travel-sore body and a befuddled brain, in no condition to savour the finest treats of Athens. Before leaving Australia, I had done something out of character. I'd purchased a two-day ticket for a hop-on-hop-off tourist bus.

These self-guided tours have proliferated in cities around the world. Multiple coaches run circular routes throughout the day, stopping at tourist sites, shopping districts, beaches and transportation hubs. They supply earphones and an audio commentary, and you can get on and off as many times as you like. If you examine the glossy booklet the driver hands you as you board, you might find the ticket entitles you to perks such as walking tours or discounted entry to tourist attractions.

If you want to be an adventurous explorer, striding away from the beaten tourist track, this isn't how to do it. But it's hard to argue against their convenience. I figured they'd help me to navigate the city on my first jet-lagged day and provide transport to some of the harder-to-reach sites on the second.

Viewing landmarks from the open-topped coach was easy, and the shiny red bus with its jaunty soundtrack and sun-drenched upper deck was a million miles away from the grimy vehicle that had shattered my life in Sri Lanka. Instead of swerving around cars that were overtaking trucks – turning a two-lane rural road into six haphazard lines of death-defying chaos – the sedate Athens coach hugged the kerb as it trundled from Hadrian's Arch and the Temple of Olympian Zeus to the ancient white marble Panathenaic Stadium, then past the National Library and the fountains of Omonia Square.

But, cheerful as it was, the tour was *so* not the way to recover my passion for travel. Passive and disconnected, I was trapped in the mundane. And it wasn't helping me get my bearings, either. To do that, you need to walk. You need to climb steps, sniff the breeze, listen to the sounds of the city. You need to feel the cobbles beneath your feet and the sun's heat on your neck as you consult maps and ask for directions and take wrong turns and find your way back again.

I consoled myself that I could do all that the following day and settled into my seat to make the best of it.

The coach completed its first circuit and approached the Acropolis stop. This was where you could transfer to the Piraeus loop to visit the busy seaport that has been a transport hub for more than two thousand years. As I shrugged on my daypack, I caught sight of my watch. *Just in time for the free walking tour,* I thought. *Might as well join in. It shouldn't take long, and the exercise will be good for me.*

# CHAPTER FOUR
## ATHENS TO THE LAKE
## AND BACK

IMITRI WORE LONG TROUSERS, a collared shirt and the bus company's red patterned necktie, but his white shirtsleeves were rolled to the elbow and his bucket hat had faded to pink in the sunshine. He turned his back on the tide of people flowing towards the World Heritage-listed Acropolis and guided us up a deserted hillside path to the Prison of Socrates, three gaping cave mouths in a wall of rock.

What did I know about Socrates, or Greek philosophers in general? Not a whole lot. Just a confusion of old men in white togas, and *Eureka!* in the bathtub.

Greece's history wasn't a feature of our school curriculum when I was growing up, and all I knew about its philosophers was what I'd picked up from popular culture. My favourite author, Terry Pratchett, set his stories on a fantasy planet called the Discworld, and one of its countries, Ephebe, bears a remarkable resemblance to Ancient Greece. Pratchett's tales paint a humorous picture of Ephebe's philosophers as bickering savants squabbling over doomed experiments in logic, often involving a much-put-upon tortoise. His books *Pyramids* and *Small Gods* had influenced the way I imagined the real Greek philosophers without my even realising it. I had never considered the seriousness of the ground they were breaking, or the obstacles they faced. I'd never thought of their philosophy as a revolution.

*Plato was the student of Socrates. Or was it the other way around? And where did Aristotle fit in?* I couldn't remember. But the philosopher's prison was one of the few Athens landmarks my mother had mentioned in her journal, so it piqued my interest. Plus, the contrast between the serenity of this site and the barely controlled commotion of tourist coaches a couple of hundred metres away was profound.

Then, Dimitri brought Socrates to life.

Socrates, that smelly old rabble-rouser who didn't know when to shut up for his own good. A frog-faced troublemaker, condemned to die in 399 BCE for his lack of reverence for the gods, as well as for inciting the youth of the city to question the authority of their elders. The jury at his trial was surely one of the largest ever to pronounce the death sentence, decided by a majority of 280 votes to 220.

Socrates may have been a stirrer, but he was such an ardent disciple of the philosophies and ideals of Athens that he rejected his followers' attempts to rescue him. Out of respect for the city's laws, he swallowed the poisonous hemlock.

And here we stood, two and a half thousand years later, at the very spot where Socrates spent the night before he died.

'Well,' said Dimitri, 'not quite.'

My mother was just one of multitudes of tourists who have stood on this patch of gravel-strewn earth, gazing at these shallow caves in the belief that this was where Socrates passed his last night. Archaeologists, though, say this is unlikely. Current theories place his imprisonment within the Ancient Agora, where you can see the cells in the ruins of a jail. Still, the maps, tour guides, signposts and guidebooks refer to these grille-covered hollows as the Prison of Socrates – until you get to the site itself. Here, Dimitri pointed out, crooking his fingers in the air, the information board describes them as 'the "Prison of Socrates"'. The awkward punctuation says it all.

The caves were typical of ancient dwellings in the area, and the tradition that Socrates spent his last night here was groundless. But they did have a noteworthy history in more recent times: the people of Athens hid their cultural treasures there when the city was occupied by Nazi Germany in the 1940s.

Next, Dimitri took us to the chapel of Saint Dimitri Loumbardiaris, so nearby that my mum's group of devout tourists was certain to have paused there. After trying the locked front door, he shepherded us around the back of the little church, urging us to feel the geometric shapes, tiny apertures and occasional faux fossils embedded in its stone walls. In Dimitri's Greek accent, the saint's name reminded me of the English word 'bombardier'. It was satisfying to learn the moniker originated with a miraculous bolt of lightning that struck down Yusuf, the seventeenth-century Turkish commander who was trying to bomb the church from the nearby Acropolis. I wondered whether my mother's fingers had explored these same contours while she listened to the same story, of a heavenly bombardier striking down an earthly one.

A short walk led to the Pnyx, the site of the famed democratic assemblies of Ancient Greece. Dimitri split the group in two. Some of us roamed the grassy parkland, while speaking in conversational tones with those who stayed standing at the stone *bema*, the orator's platform set against a rocky outcrop. The acoustics were outstanding for what is – and was – an open field. This was how a single speaker in the crowd could make himself heard among the thousands at the open-air gatherings on the Pnyx all those centuries ago. And it would have been a man. Women had little part in that democracy.

On the way to, from, and around the Pnyx, our group of six passed two other people. By contrast, the hill of the Acropolis, just minutes away, was teeming with tourists.

A charismatic archaeologist and historian, Dimitri held us bound in a state of unrelenting fascination. When he returned to the bus stop to pick up a dozen people for his next talk, I abandoned my plans for the afternoon and tagged along. So did everyone else from the first tour, even the officious German backpacker who had only one day in Athens and had plotted a complicated itinerary to cram as much in as he could.

For five hours, Dimitri ushered us around the outskirts of the Acropolis. He spoke of mythology and the politics of Ancient Greece, of wars and architecture, of art and religion, of Leonidas and Saint Paul. His enthusiasm was as visible as it was infectious, his wiry body bristling with passion for his subject as he spoke. On our path down into the cobbled lanes of Plaka, he had us perch on the hillside steps under a shady tree as he enthralled us with tales of Alexander the Great. Arguably the most prolific military campaigner of the ancient world, Alexander created an empire that stretched from Greece and the modern-day Republic of North Macedonia all the way to India before he died at the ripe old age of thirty-two.

When the tour ended in Monastiraki Square, Dimitri pointed the way to the Ancient Agora, a massive complex he had shown us from above. Inspired by his account, I set out on the ten-minute walk to the agora's majestic Temple of Hephaestus, the ugly Greek god of artisans, metals, fire, volcanoes and – most important for me, a Smith by name – ironworkers. It was Hephaestus who assisted in the birth of the city's patron goddess, Athena, setting her free from Zeus's forehead with a wallop from his mighty axe. Or possibly his hammer. With or without a wedge used to split his head open like a block of firewood. It might even have been someone else who struck the blow – there are that many versions of the legend.

The thirty-acre agora, the commercial centre of antiquity, was criss-crossed with stone foundations poking through yellow grassland, and dotted with reconstructed temples and the edifices of ancient government. It had a statue-lined stoa, a fourth-century BCE water clock, the remains of libraries, streets and an aqueduct. The tiny tenth-century Church of the Holy Apostles, at the edge of the sprawling site, commemorated Saint Paul's sermons delivered in this very marketplace a couple of decades after the death of Jesus Christ.

Much to my gleeful delight, there were even tortoises clambering around the ruins of the current contender for the cells where Socrates would have spent his last night. I couldn't wait to share a picture on social media for fellow Discworld aficionados who might pick up on the reference to Pratchett's Ephebian philosophers.

Dimitri was a skilled storyteller, a true son of the Ancient Greek orators. He'd transformed the day I'd been prepared to write off to jet lag into something fabulous. Instead of the twenty minutes of superficiality I'd expected, his tour – a token extra included in the price of a bus ticket – gave me the tools to explore Athens, and woke in me a fervent drive to soak up every drop that Greece had to offer.

~ ~ ~

Day Two's breakfast offerings were identical to the previous morning's, but I was content with the wholesome fare. Yesterday's breakfast had sustained me through ten hours out in the enervating heat, most of them on foot, until an early dinner at an excellent souvlaki joint recommended by Dimitri. It must have been the olives – unappealing little things – that did the trick. I spooned another two onto my plate.

It was the final day of my hop-on-hop-off bus ticket and there were still two circuits to cover. I got to the stop with enough time to pop across the road to see Hadrian's Arch and the Temple of Olympian Zeus.

The temple took over three hundred years to build and was renowned as the largest in Greece, but it stood for barely more than a century before it was pillaged by invaders in 267 CE and fell into disrepair.

It was the second-century Roman Emperor Hadrian who had completed the temple's construction. Now, *there* was a man who liked an ambitious building project. He is better known for Hadrian's Wall in northern England, but his monumental archway in Athens was just as blatant a marking of his territory. The side facing the Parthenon bore the inscription, 'This is Athens, the ancient city of Theseus'. Turning his back on that minotaur-slaying hero king of long-ago Athens, Hadrian had the other side, facing the Temple of Olympian Zeus, inscribed, 'This is the city of Hadrian and not of Theseus'.

Mum's diary said she 'Wandered around Temple of Zeus' and, puzzlingly, 'Sat on throne' but I could only take a few photos of its remaining columns through the fence railings before boarding the first coach for the coastal Beaches-Riviera route. My destination was its furthest point, Lake Vouliagmeni.

The word *vouliagmeni* means 'sunken' and this lake, about twenty kilometres south of Athens, was once hidden in a large cavern. The roof collapsed hundreds of years ago and much of the lake now lies open to the air, although it extends into caves deep underground, fed by brackish subterranean currents. Thousands of delicate fish swarm through the mineral-rich water, in search of toes to nibble.

The lake is a constant, comfortable temperature and rumoured to have health benefits for bathers, and its fish provide a tickling pedicure while you float. The shore is well designed for day-trippers, with showers and lockers, deckchairs and waiters bearing cocktail menus, but it wasn't crowded. The water felt delicious in the sweltering heat and

I would have been happy to relax here until late afternoon, surrounded by families chatting in Greek. But with only three full days in Athens, I had to ration my time. After two hours of swimming and refraining from drinking cocktails, I packed up my things and headed to the bus. Just as when I arrived, no one else got on or off at this stop. It was a mystery: *Where do all the tourists go when they descend from the Acropolis?*

On the bus ride to the lake, the recorded commentary had mentioned an attractive church as the location of a failed assassination attempt on Greece's King George in 1898. The church of Agios Sostis, or Christ the Saviour, sat in a tiny oasis of trees amid a concrete jungle. It wasn't adjacent to a bus stop, merely a point of interest as we sped down the motorway, but it had caught my attention.

If I left the bus on the return trip to Athens, I calculated, I could walk twenty sweaty minutes to the church, then cross through a pedestrian underpass and trudge back in the blinding sunshine to catch the Piraeus loop bus on the other side of the busy road. The trek was an unpleasant trade-off for only a few minutes inside, but it was worth it.

The church was built in a palette of pink and white, offset by the colours of its tiles: turquoise decorated its walls, terracotta topped its octagonal domed roof. It wasn't quite empty, and I was glad I'd remembered to cover my shoulders with a shawl. Three elderly women dressed in black were arranging flowers and there were a few parishioners scattered about, kissing icons or praying in the pews under gilded chandeliers. Light streamed in from high windows, gleaming through the iron framework – pillars and arches wrought into the shape of climbing foliage, a lacy filigree that was strong enough to support the weight of the building.

I'd imagined the assassination attempt taking place while the king was at prayer, but in fact he was not attending church at the time. The church wasn't even there.

King George and Princess Maria were in a carriage on their way home from a seaside trip when two gunmen attacked. The king and his daughter escaped unharmed, although both a servant and a horse suffered injuries. The assailants were caught and later beheaded in Nafplio on the Peloponnese peninsula.

To give thanks for the king's wellbeing, the municipal council erected a church at the site of the ambush, making use of an unusual existing structure. The building had served as the Greek pavilion at a magnificent world's fair, the event which hosted the first Olympic Games outside Greece. When the 1900 Paris Exposition closed, they dismantled the brick pavilion and shipped it to Athens, where it became this pretty church.

King George's reprieve from assassination was temporary. In 1913, near the White Tower in Thessaloniki, a bullet would finish the job. A decade later, his grandson, Prince Philip, was born on the island of Corfu and grew up to become the husband of Queen Elizabeth II, monarch not only of the United Kingdom, but also of my new home, Australia.

~ ~ ~

The drive around Piraeus was pleasant enough, although you can only take in so much of the harbour from the upper deck of an open-topped bus. My first encounter with the name of this seaport, which has served Athens for twenty-five centuries, was as a child absorbed in Goscinny and Uderzo's graphic novels. In *Asterix at the Olympic Games*, a bemused Obelix asked Getafix, 'Who is Piraeus?' (Later, he asked, 'Who is this Thea Cropolis?' My mother sat me on her knee to explain the joke.)

Back in Athens, and ravenous, I retraced the previous day's steps to a restaurant Dimitri had recommended as his mother's favourite. What a disappointment. The food was lukewarm and greasy, stale and overpriced, and I left two-thirds of it congealing on my plate. *Perhaps they pull out all the stops for their Greek regulars, and pull out something quite different for us tourists.* The Alfa was good though. I'm not usually a beer drinker, but now and then, it hits the spot.

A thunderstorm was brewing, giving a glimmer of hope that the weather might cool. To walk off the unaccustomed lunchtime lager, which had gone straight to my head, I left

tourism central and headed towards Filopappou Hill, also
known as the Hill of the Muses.

~ ~ ~

This is where I need to make a confession about my mother's
diary. It is a precious thing to have, a tangible link to my mum,
who died when I was in my twenties. The truth, though, is
that I found it disturbing.

I can only hope a great deal is lost in translation. My
mother wrote her tiny journal in the most abbreviated
fashion, covering two overseas trips with blank pages to
spare. Typical entries range from the mundane: 'To bed. Mom
chesty' to the cheery: 'Dinner at carvery, fat chef and Aussie
waitress' to the cryptic: 'Plumber's friend in jar'. There is the
evocative: 'Bought grapes at roadside – weighed with stones'.
And the alliterative: 'Muezzin calling madly' scribbled at the
bottom of a page, recalling the glorious medley of prayer that
started my days when I lived in the United Arab Emirates.

Some of the entries, though, were disconcerting. It was as
if they'd been written by someone I'd never met.

I grinned at '6 of us drank 7 bottles of wine. Pouring
outside. Fell & hurt leg.'

'Madge bathed with us, & so to bed' triggered a naughty
chuckle. I didn't know who Madge was, but I hoped there
was a backstory about a malfunctioning shower in her hotel

room. Madge was accident-prone, after all, dropping an icon in Jerusalem, breaking her camera in Rome and falling over when they ventured into the Italian countryside. I could relate to her clumsiness, and it was a relief to read that she felt 'suddenly better during mass due to prayers' when their pilgrimage reached the Shroud of Turin.

But I was uncomfortable with 'picked up marble' at the Temple of Olympian Zeus. And appalled by 'To mt of 7 muses. Tried to push over temple.'

This 'temple' must have been the impressive memorial to Filopappou that crests the Hill of the Muses. I could see my mother, like countless other tourists, pocketing a pebble from an archaeological site without a second thought. But I couldn't imagine her trying to topple a temple unprovoked. I guessed a disreputable tour guide – this *was* the 1970s – had commented on the strength of the construction and encouraged the group to give it a shove. Still, this might explain why a sturdy, and rather ugly, fence stood between me and the monument.

# CHAPTER FIVE
## ICONS OF ATHENS

**B**Y THE TIME I descended Filopappou Hill, the beer had sweated its way out of my system and the blasting heat had cooled by a degree or three. There'd be no better opportunity to visit the Acropolis.

I trudged up yet another incline, tarrying a while at two grand performance spaces of old: the Odeon of Herodes Atticus and the Theatre of Dionysus. Thunder rumbled with the sweet promise of rain as I passed a crudely carved stone sign forbidding singing, making loud noises or taking 'moving pictures' without written permission from the archaeological service. I resolved to restrain myself on all three counts.

Above Athens, golden shafts of light pierced boiling clouds that darkened from shining silver to a deep, brooding grey. The temperature dipped a fraction further and, as I crossed the threshold of the gateway into the Acropolis, one or two fat drops fell from the heavens.

The Parthenon is by far the best-known monument of the Acropolis – so much so that many make the mistake of using the two names interchangeably. But the Parthenon is a single temple, while the word 'acropolis' refers to the entire hilltop campus. Coming from the Greek *akro* (peak or edge) and *polis* (city), it means an urban precinct perched on high ground. There are many acropolises in Greece, often dedicated to the gods or serving as fortresses, though only the one in Athens is awarded the capital letter 'A'.

Built to honour the virgin goddess Athena, the Parthenon has stood for two thousand five hundred years. It has served as a Christian church, a Muslim mosque, a treasury and, to its own peril, an armoury.

There have been three great threats to the Parthenon's existence in the last five hundred years. In the seventeenth century, Venetians bombarding the Turkish-held Acropolis ignited a store of gunpowder, setting off a massive explosion inside the ancient temple. In the nineteenth, its treasures were pillaged for museums around the world, most notably by the infamous Lord Elgin for the British Museum. Then there was the twentieth-century damage caused by *nephos*, the smoggy air pollution that hung over Athens until government controls reduced fuel emissions in the city.

Nevertheless, it remains a radiant beacon glowing over Athens, and, for many, it is the symbol of the Acropolis. In my opinion, though, it is not its only jewel. So, which is the crowning gem, more lovely still than the magnificent Parthenon?

Maybe the Erechtheion with its Porch of the Caryatids, stately stone maidens supporting its roof on their noble heads? They stand proud, their hair braided and their bodies draped in soft garments of gleaming marble. And while it is clear they are sisters – in blood, stone or spirit – each is her own woman. Her individuality shines through the set of her shoulders, the tilt of her leg, the folds of her dress. Their faces have been damaged by the centuries, their arms lost, but they are strong women, all.

Or perhaps the temple of Athena Nike, tiny but of graceful proportions? The cult statue locked inside this shrine was known as *Apteros Niki*, the Wingless Victory. One legend tells that the Ancient Athenians had captured the goddess Nike, stripped her of her wings so Victory could never forsake the city, and imprisoned her in this sad marble box.

Apart from the striking architecture posing under thunderous skies, my memories of the Acropolis are a series of more personal snapshots:

A sleeping cat snuggled between the barrel and balls of a rusting cannon, basking in their metallic warmth.

The beauty of a construction crane silhouetted against seething clouds, behind the age-old columns of the Parthenon.

And the olive tree – or, at least, *an* olive tree – gifted to Athens by the grey-eyed goddess, Athena. So grateful were the citizens for its wood, shade, oil and pungent fruit that they named their city for Athena rather than her rival Poseidon, the god of the sea, who'd offered the townspeople a spring of salty water. It is said that the olive growing near the Porch of the Caryatids can be traced back to the original tree of the legend.

~ ~ ~

Hoping to get a sense of how the landmarks I'd seen combined into one cityscape, I hopped onto the bus for a final loop around Athens. I hadn't bargained on this being the last coach for the evening, though. It stopped at Syntagma Square, a lot further from my bed than where I had climbed aboard. Still, it only took half an hour of vigorous walking to get to my hotel, and, on the way, I did get to watch an iconic rite: the Changing of the Guard.

Imagine statuesque soldiers moving in slow motion under the darkening sky, each exaggerated extension of a white-stockinged leg ending with a stylised flick of a pompom-adorned foot. It would be a mistake to write the ritual off as pantomime. The *Evzones*, this elite unit of the Greek army, has a proud history. While their uniform may appear whimsical to a foreign eye, it harks back to the outfits worn by early nineteenth-century Greek rebels during their war for independence from the Ottomans. The *foustanélla* of their full ceremonial uniform – a kilt-like garment with four hundred pleats symbolising four hundred years of Turkish occupation – is sewn from thirty metres of snow-white cloth and is apparently a bugger to iron. Their nail-studded shoes with fluffy black pompoms weigh around three kilograms a pair.

The *Evzones* treat their job of guarding the Hellenic Parliament building, housed within the Old Royal Palace on Syntagma Square, as a solemn undertaking. They stand motionless at the Tomb of the Unknown Soldier, without a flicker of facial expression. An Athens tourism website reported that, when a Molotov cocktail destroyed a guardhouse during a violent protest in 2001, the soldier remained at his post, his uniform scorched and smoking, until he received the order to move away.

As for those pompoms on their shoes, why should they be considered any more ludicrous than the enormous pompoms I mean bearskins – on the heads of the Queen's Guard at Buckingham Palace?

Despite my hunger after an active day and the unsatisfying lunch left on my plate, I strode past the tacky eateries in the bustling tourist district. Just three minutes from my lodgings, I came across Kalamaki Bar, its tables filled with Greek diners. The waiter grinned when I asked for *krasi*, using the first word of Greek I'd memorised after the basic social niceties. I guessed from his smile that I'd mangled the syllables, but it worked like a charm. A glass of crisp white wine appeared, along with the tender beef skewer and tasty spinach, fig and walnut salad I'd ordered by pointing at the bilingual menu and mispronouncing *parakaló*.

And, as my mother would have recorded, so to bed.

~ ~ ~

TripAdvisor reviews recommended I let the hotel know in advance whether I preferred a quiet room or one with a view. I opted for silence, so they gave me a solidly built room on the first floor, its only window looking out into the base of a lightwell. This suited me just fine. Apart from sleeping, any little time spent in my hotel room would be because I needed a break from the sensory overload of the city. A view might be pleasant, but silence is priceless.

The room's entrance opened into a vestibule with a fridge and two sturdy doors, one leading to the bathroom and the other to the bedroom. This was another plus. I could hang the 'Do Not Disturb' sign on the bedroom doorknob, hiding my belongings spread out in chaos all over the furniture, and still have my bathroom cleaned every day.

Frequent servicing of the bathroom was important as, in Greece, you have to put used toilet paper into the garbage bin instead of flushing it away. This is because of the small diameter of the older pipes that make up much of the Greek sanitation system. The narrow sewers simply cannot cope with clogging quantities of paper. It can be a distasteful practice at first, to those of us who aren't accustomed to it, but it soon becomes second nature.

~ ~ ~

Day Three was a gentle day. It was the downtime I needed to find a laundromat and work out how to travel to my next destination. Between errands, I continued my discovery of Athens.

The National Garden was a shady haven from the heat. This thirty-eight-acre park was commissioned in 1838 by Amalia, the first queen of modern Greece. Eighty-two years later, it was the downfall of King Alexander, who was bitten by a pet monkey while walking his dog there. The wound turned septic and the young king died three weeks later, aged just twenty-seven.

The garden's twisting avenues were an explorer's delight, but the cramped aviaries filled with birds saddened me, and the elusive central lake left me bewildered. I knew it existed but, as if in a dream, every path I wandered seemed to detour away from it.

I abandoned the garden in favour of the Bathhouse of the Winds, fifteen minutes' walk away, where a lone ticket-seller welcomed me into an otherwise empty building. For at least three hundred years, from an unknown date during the Ottoman occupation until the mid-twentieth century, this public hammam served the people of Athens. In the late nineteenth century, the bathhouse was enlarged to allow separate wings for male and female patrons. Until then, men and women visited the baths at specified times, to avoid the sexes meeting at their ablutions.

The Bathhouse of the Winds was named after a remarkable tower in the nearby Roman Agora. The Tower of the Winds, built from Pentelic marble around 50 BCE, features a wind vane, water clock, eight sundials and a striking stone frieze depicting the gods of the winds. It is said to be the oldest meteorological station in the world. Over the centuries, it has inspired reverence in the changing citizenry of Athens, serving as an Eastern Orthodox bell tower in early Christian times, and as a dervish tekke when the city was under Ottoman rule. If I allowed myself to muddle the epochs, I could imagine a glorious scene, with the billowing white skirts of dervish robes whirling to the peal of church bells.

Behind the tower, sixty-eight latrines sat in a companionable square, set close together to make it easy to pass around a communal sponge. *Did women have access to these oh-so-public toilets?* The silent query slid through my mind. *Or, in this bodily function as in so much else, were we expected to stay at home?*

The first time I'd encountered toilets like these was in an archaeological site in Tunisia. It was February 2000, six months after my mum died, and my first solo trip. A few days later, I ventured out to find a contemporary hammam. That quest for authenticity ended in my scrubbing the back of a motherly stranger who took pity on me for not having my own soap.

Bathhouses have fascinated me ever since. So it was a joy to spend two euros and forty-five blissful minutes wandering this restored hammam, imagining a time when its cool rooms were clouded by steam. A downloadable app on my phone gave glimpses into the lives of the women who had bathed here, but left me wondering about those who had toiled long, strenuous hours in its punishing heat.

There were a few clues to their identity. The illustrations showed African women working in the hammams, and the app quoted a writer whose name I couldn't decipher. When he was a young child on the Greek island of Kos in the 1930s, his mother had taken him with her to bathe. He described 'the bathhouse women, half naked and skeletal, with hands roughened by the water, and sometimes with strong negroid characteristics.' But how these women came from the continent of my birth to labour in such harsh conditions remained a mystery.

On the way out, I chuckled at the euphemism of an exhibited latrine in the floor being labelled 'the bathroom'. *Hammam* is Turkish for bathhouse, so the entire building was technically a bathroom.

My last stop of the day, the Acropolis Museum, was tremendous. It is a modernist structure that seems to be set at an awkward angle until you gaze out at the Parthenon, which it mirrors with precision. The museum is in perfect alignment with the ancient temple.

The uppermost level of the museum houses the Parthenon's original stone friezes and statuary and, if you're happy to swim against the current of those taking the more obvious route, it's an excellent place to start. This is where you can view the temple's huge adornments up close, with the many gaps in the original yellowed marble filled with bright, white replicas. The contrast in colour drives home the scale of the damage done by Elgin and his counterparts from other lands. This nineteenth-century removal of loot for the benefit of other countries' collections wasn't pilfering. It was hardcore plunder. And although there might be some self-deluding comfort in claiming that the relocation of the missing antiquities was a rescue mission rather than vandalism, it's difficult to sustain this argument in the presence of the pieces that still stand, cherished and protected, within sight of their home.

As a bit of a museum geek, myself, this gave me much to ponder. Using the free Wi-Fi, I logged in to Facebook to post:

11 September 2016
Wow. That Lord Elgin. He sure stole a lot of marbles.

I wondered what my mother might have thought about Elgin and the Parthenon marbles. *Would she see any link between her picking up a piece of stone from the ground, and Elgin hacking sculptures away from the temple façade?* Or was I the one being too judgemental? *I suppose it was just a pebble.* But I worked alongside archaeologists in my youth. I knew how important it was to leave artefacts untouched.

Mum was a good person. I probably got my strongest values – honesty, kindness and respect – from her. But when it came to the detail of our ethical, religious and socio-political beliefs, we shared little common ground. Mum's comments on my life choices would end with the casual throwaway, 'But, of course, you have no morals.' I'd like to think we could chat about whether the Parthenon Marbles should return to their home, but if our track record was anything to go by, any serious discussion would end in sullen disagreement. *What's done is done. It would be better not to mention that marble fragment at all, in case she feels attacked.*

When I realised my thoughts had switched to the present tense, mapping a pathway through a complex conversation that could never happen, I pulled her diary from my backpack. The early pages recorded her first overseas trip, to England in 1974, and, *Yes, she visited the British Museum.* But the only object she mentioned was the Rosetta Stone. Frustrated, I zipped her journal back into the bag.

As I worked my way down the museum's levels, I came across five of the Erechtheion's original caryatids keeping watch from a mezzanine that floated above the galleries. Elgin carted away their sixth stone sister long ago. Having witnessed the extent of his pillage, I was amazed he had left five maidens untouched. What I'd seen at the Acropolis the previous day were replicas holding up the ceiling of their famous porch.

From behind all the old stone came a glimpse of bright plastic: an intricate Lego model of the Acropolis. Constructed from more than 120,000 bricks, it featured miniature caryatids holding up a Lego porch roof next to Athena's olive tree. It even showed the statuary on a tiny Parthenon's pediments, topped with an ornament mimicking the massive, fern-like sculpture I'd examined upstairs just a few minutes before.

A closer look revealed Lego figurines representing a mishmash of periods. There were actors performing in the Theatre of Dionysus, and a minuscule Elton John at his grand piano in the great-arched Odeon of Herodes Atticus. Here was the bull-headed Minotaur, and there the fourth-century BCE philosopher Diogenes the Cynic, reputed to have lived in a barrel, although it was more likely a large clay jar called a pithos. A skeleton lurked in the depths of the hill, safe from the trowels of treasure hunters, while Lord Elgin carried away the marbles and present-day tourists flocked to a souvlaki stand. It was a work of art, and I smiled to read it came from Australia's Brickman team of Lego crafters.

My social media photos of this masterpiece elicited two comments. One was from my thirty-something nephew, Christopher: 'NOW I'm jealous.' The other was from my sister, Jenny: 'Fifteen years ago right now we were in Lima. You sure do get around.'

Christopher's words made me laugh, but Jenny's catapulted me into a rush of memory and emotion: three sisters on foot, a rite of passage that went off the rails, and a taxi hurtling through the Peruvian Andes.

# CHAPTER SIX
## ATHENS TO MONEMVASIA

SOME PEOPLE DISPARAGE TRAVEL guides such as the *Lonely Planet*, my personal favourite, and those who use them. They argue that guidebooks spoon-feed every traveller an identical experience. But why would I squander thousands of dollars and days of uncomfortable travel, investing weeks of precious vacation and, more importantly, my life, only to discover afterwards that I missed something exceptional because I didn't know it was there?

A guidebook also gives me a place to start with the two essentials I prefer to arrange in advance. A safe place to sleep is a priority for a woman travelling on her own, and if it can be clean, quirky, convenient and comfortable, so much the better. And I've learned to plan ahead for long-distance travel between towns – a glance at a map gives scant insight into the logistics of moving about using buses, trains and ferries.

My *Lonely Planet* doesn't kill spontaneity; it sparks it. Often, I'll set off in search of something from a passage I've read, then be side-tracked by a sound, a scent or a splash of colour that catches my eye. Soon, I take a step off the tourist track and slip into a memory-making moment of taste or texture or simple wonder. Far from forcing me into a one-size-fits-all travel package, a bit of research gives me the freedom to 'follow my nose' – as my grandmother used to say – with the greatest pleasure.

~ ~ ~

Monemvasia is an island joined to the Peloponnese peninsula by a narrow causeway. It looks like an immense Rock jutting out of the sea, and that has become its moniker. Greeks, Franks, Venetians and Turks have squabbled over the territory since its first inhabitants sought safety there in the sixth century, with each victor shoring up the Rock's natural defences against the next potential predator.

The walled settlement of Monemvasia is called the Kastro. Its medieval Lower Town is invisible from the adjacent mainland, making it a near-perfect refuge, and you're unlikely to spot the ruins of the even more fortified Upper City from afar unless you know exactly where to look. The Kastro's entrance is an L-shaped portal designed to hide the town from intruders unless they penetrate deep inside. This forbidding gateway gives the island its formal name: *moni* means 'single', *emvasia* refers to the only access point through which invaders could attack. Behind it lies a Byzantine paradise.

Before consulting my travel bible, I'd never heard of Monemvasia. Now, I was on my way.

Finding Kifissos, one of the intercity coach terminals in Athens, involved a Metro ride and a walk to an obscure bus stop, then cramming myself and my suitcase into a swaying vehicle packed with people heading to the terminal and beyond. I overestimated how long this would take and ended up arriving two hours early. This gave me more than enough time to navigate the terminal, buy my ticket and sip an iced soft drink in the cafeteria while flipping through the pages of my guidebook.

Killing time in a bus station is an ideal situation to observe desperate entrepreneurship in action. The industry here was the hawking of small packets of tissues, the kind you can buy at supermarkets in larger packs of a dozen or so. At Kifissos, three women each worked alone, approaching travellers in a polite attempt to sell tissues at two packets for a euro. One of the women was as neatly dressed as if she were about to attend a business meeting, another was in shabby clothing, and the third wore a nondescript outfit that fell between these extremes. They had a well-chosen target market, but I only saw one sale.

I didn't need tissues. I had left Australia with a dozen packets in my bag and was barely halfway through the first, but I bought some anyway.

Here's the thing. Greece is a country that has endured significant economic hardship, with high unemployment and austerity measures causing wages to plummet. And yet, it has aided multitudes of refugees – the same refugees turned away by much wealthier nations, including Australia.

There were many people on the streets of Athens, both Greek and not Greek, looking for ways to support themselves. Some would have been qualified professionals, brought down by circumstances beyond their control. Others may never have had the opportunities for education and employment many of us take for granted. Still others would have been there by choice, flourishing in the informal economy.

If we're rich enough to travel the world, surely we can spare a few coins for those working hard to make an honest living. Don't need tissues right now? Consider buying a packet for later. Drop some change in the hat of the street performer who added colour to our commute, give the waiter a few euros, leave a bit extra for the woman with the nasty job of cleaning the public toilets. We may not think of ourselves as wealthy and, by some standards, we might even be travelling on the cheap. But we are a lot luckier than that elderly lady who's on her feet all day in the crippling heat, making a small profit through the sale of a few packets of tissues and hoping it will be enough to feed her grandchildren.

I'm not above feeling irritated at a persistent vendor, and I am not naïve. I know about street crime and begging syndicates and the misuse of children to make money. I won't allow these horrible realities to rob me of my own humanity, though. And there are always opportunities to contribute to the small-scale local economy.

~ ~ ~

People clustered on one side of the bus, shoving bags into the luggage compartment. Passengers climbed up through the door on the other.

I hadn't realised the tickets to Monemvasia included allocated seating. Because I'd arrived so early, the efficient ticket-seller had, without consulting me, given me the best seat in the house. Depending on your perspective, of course. From mine, it was the death seat. The exact one where I sat on that fateful trip in Sri Lanka. Front right window seat. The difference, in a left-hand drive vehicle, was that I didn't even have the driver between me and the windscreen. There'd be a splendid view. I hoped I wouldn't shatter it.

I'm pretty sure I was the only person on the bus scrabbling about for my seatbelt.

It was a long ride to Monemvasia, passing through varied landscapes from industrial suburbs to vineyards and olive groves. But there was no doubt about the moment we crossed over onto the Peloponnese, the massive peninsula, west of Athens, that looks like a hand stretching down towards the Mediterranean Sea.

The Isthmus of Corinth is the strip of ground that connects this peninsula to the rest of the mainland. For thousands of years, humans have sought ways to transport their ships across the isthmus, from the Gulf of Corinth in the north to the Saronic Gulf in the south. The ancients considered a canal but encountered such insurmountable engineering obstacles that they resorted to alternative solutions, like hauling sea vessels along a stone track or rolling them across logs.

Millennia later, in 1893, the six-and-a-half-kilometre Corinth Canal was excavated. Now, more than a hundred years after its construction, this deep channel flashed past the window of our fast-moving vehicle. Although I'd been looking out for it, I wasn't prepared for the verticality of this narrow wound slashed through the land. Before I could inhale through the sudden shock, it was gone. I'd have to take a closer look on the return trip in a few days' time.

We travelled swiftly over the Peloponnese, with scheduled stops at the major bus stations of Corinth Isthmus, Tripoli and Sparta to collect passengers or let them disembark. There was one brief cafeteria stop, but the food on offer was an unappetising array of dense pastries, displayed next to racks of pre-packaged snacks. They all ranged in colour from beige to brown, and I decided to wait. The toilets were even more dismal, but needs must.

Back onboard, a sprinkle of droplets danced across the windows as the coach accelerated, and I remembered how

I'd relished the fine rain that day, ten years before, on the Sri Lankan bus. I would have been happier, now, to travel a little less swiftly on this drizzle-slick road curving through the hills. Still, the trip had already taken several hours, and the sooner we arrived, the sooner I could enjoy a late lunch with a glass of chilled *krasi*.

As the journey progressed with no catastrophes, my phobia's grip slackened. To occupy the slow hours, I searched for signs printed in both Greek and English alphabets, comparing the letters in the place names. As the characters became more familiar, I focused on those in only Greek script. Each line of symbols I could decode into a recognisable word was a small victory. *Niki*, I reminded myself, picturing the victorious goddess Nike in a pair of athletic shoes.

Not only did I have a fine view through the windscreen, I also had a clear line of sight to the driver. This wasn't a problem until he started rummaging around in his satchel with one hand. Out came a thick stack of pages, the likes of which I hadn't seen in years: perforated dot matrix printing paper, complete with little holes running along its edges. The type where you can tear the sheets apart along the perforations or leave them connected in a long concertina that can be opened out and refolded at any page, like a mishandled map.

That's a clumsy process at best. Certainly when done with one hand – no, wait, make that two hands on the printout, with just an elbow resting on the steering wheel – while driving a loaded bus through rolling hills.

Once he had arranged the pile of paper to his satisfaction, I unclenched my hands from the armrests. But then it was time for him to consult the document, a lengthy list or travel manifest of some kind. With up to two slow seconds – I counted them – perusing the printout for each quick flick of his eyes back to the road.

My own eyes darted from the driver to the road ahead, to the movie playing in my mind. You'd think my flashback would have focused on Sri Lanka but, perhaps because of Jenny's Facebook comment the day before reminding me of our stay in Lima, it was a nerve-racking ride through the Andes that looped through the reel. The protagonist was a comical taxi driver, but it was the extras – cows on the mountain road, looming through the Peruvian twilight – that provided the drama.

Pulling myself back to the present, I put myself on watch duty, preparing to yell out a warning if I spotted any hazards in our path. Luckily, passing traffic was almost non-existent and we reached Sparta, the last sizeable town before Monemvasia, without me calling embarrassing attention to myself.

While most of the passengers filed out of the coach, I consoled myself that it should only be an hour or so until we reached Monemvasia. I'd estimated this by measuring distances on the map between thumb and forefinger, then comparing the time it took to travel from one town to another. What I hadn't known, though, was that our vehicle would undergo an invisible transformation in Sparta. No longer a regional intercity coach, it became a local bus winding its lazy way down the hand-shaped peninsula's Laconia finger, picking people up in tiny village squares and dropping off the few remaining passengers from Athens, often seemingly in the middle of nowhere.

The region showcased the most beautiful scenery I had yet seen in Greece, with golden grasses peeping through green trees and the harsh magnificence of grey stone. Plus, it offered an unexpected gift: glimpses into village life. But the trip had been wearing and any hope that the meal I so keenly anticipated could reasonably be called lunch, even a late one, was eroding. There was a change in drivers at a random spot on the side of a road, and all my fellow travellers got off at various points along the route until I was the last lonely passenger. It was hours before the bus finally arrived in Gefyra, the gateway to Monemvasia.

Gefyra's bus station was just a low bench in front of a tiny office with a locked front door. There was no one about in the late afternoon sunshine, so I crossed the road to a chemist and asked the young pharmacist about the shuttle bus to Monemvasia. Just then, an older woman entered. Perhaps she was a regular customer, or a colleague; either way, it was clear the two women were on good terms. In accented

English, the new arrival explained that I'd missed the shuttle. 'It will come again in half an hour. Are you travelling alone?' Barely waiting for an answer, she bustled me outside to her elderly station wagon and insisted on going out of her way to chauffeur me across the causeway and around the Rock to the Kastro's imposing entrance, beyond which no cars could pass.

With only two exceptions, the people I met in Greece were warm, welcoming and eager to help me in any way they could.

~ ~ ~

The charming Malvasia Hotel was quite different from any other hotel I've known. For a start, it wasn't all in one place. Its reception area was a lovely self-contained shopfront on the footpath leading from the formidable entry into the Kastro – although the word 'shopfront' does little justice to Monemvasia's gorgeous restaurants, boutiques and stores, built from honey-coloured stone and brimming with Byzantine character. The hotel's individual bedrooms were scattered through several buildings a few hundred metres further along this path.

Although I'm not an extravagant packer, carrying my suitcase over the uneven cobbles was a lot harder than pulling it along flat surfaces on its neat little wheels. It was tougher still when the handle broke.

Thankfully, my hotel was one of the few that didn't require a steep climb from the Kastro entrance. And my room was enchanting. Room Fourteen was the hotel's cheapest, the smallest of a handful of rooms without their own private terrace or sea view. I badly wanted to stay on the Rock itself rather than in cheaper, mainland Gefyra, and Room Fourteen made this possible without breaking the bank. It was a cosy chamber with a vaulted, stonework ceiling, steps leading up to a bathroom carved into the natural rock, and a wooden door opening onto the cobbled street. It was like a room from a fairy tale.

Energised by a quick shower, I was soon braving the heat to find supper. After all, Greek food was a key attraction in travelling here, along with the language, history and landscape.

It wasn't quite dinnertime, but the first place I ventured inside offered a toasted cheese and ham sandwich with a glass of wine. I'd imagined something more elaborate for my first meal in this oasis of azure waters and terracotta tiles. But it would be quick and, with luck, it wouldn't be long before I could collapse into bed in my air-conditioned room to gather my strength for the next day. And it turned out the cheese toastie arrived with a side of potato crisps, and the wine was served with small hunks of bread and generous chunks of hard, parmesan-like cheese.

After this substantial snack and a short stroll, though, my body started to send me urgent messages. It was begging for something fresh. I'd eaten pretty much nothing but carbohydrates with cheese all day, and the previous day had also been rich in carbs. The sandwich had been filling, but I craved something else. Maybe a salad? Oh, and another glass of wine would go down nicely, too.

At the next restaurant, I asked for a menu.

Yes, they had salad. Greek salad. It's strange that menus throughout the country offered 'Greek salad'. You'd think that here it would just be 'salad'.

And yes, they had wine, which they sold by the bottle. This seemed excessive, given that I'd already had a glass.

'No problem,' the man at the door assured me. 'You take what you don't drink to hotel.' Perfect! I could have something light to eat now, and, afterwards, I could sip a nightcap in bed with my book, with the remains of the bottle saved for the following evening.

Well, the salad was crunchy and appetising, but it wasn't light. It was enough for a small family and far more than I could eat in one sitting. Greek salad in Greece is the same as Greek salad everywhere else, except for one significant difference: instead of a few small cubes of feta tossed throughout the salad, an enormous slab of the white sheep's cheese rests atop the other ingredients of green capsicum pepper and cucumber, red onion and tomato, and masses of black Kalamata olives. I usually picked the olives out of my salad, but this time, despite being unable to finish the bowl, I consumed a fair number of them. I'd driven past the road to Kalamata on the way from Athens, after all, and one should make an effort.

You know what? They weren't bad.

# CHAPTER SEVEN
## BASIL, BOOKS
## AND MONEMVASIA'S
## BYZANTINE LANEWAYS

MATCHING BOOKS WITH DESTINATIONS is one of my favourite travel activities. And what better place to enjoy a story than in the land that inspired Aesop to tell his fables and ancient bards to sing of heroes and the gods?

As soon as I'd decided on the trip, I pestered friends to help me compile a list of books set in Greece. I powered my way through those I could borrow from the local library and downloaded a selection onto an e-reader. Paperbacks are my first love, but you can't beat electronic books for lightweight travel.

Grant, a friend from high school, recommended *Things Can Only Get Feta* by Marjory McGinn. The author was a Scottish-Australian journalist who'd moved to Greece as the country was sliding into economic crisis, and she gave an amusing account of how she settled on the Peloponnese with her husband and their charismatic Jack Russell terrier. Despite its serious themes, her story provided a little light relief: the other books on my list, excellent as they were, were set in landscapes of civil war and Nazi occupation, despair and famine, and exhausting mythological struggles. It just so happened that I'd started *Things Can Only Get Feta* on my last day in Athens, and it was a delight, when I took my glass of wine to bed and opened my e-book, to find the next chapter was set in Monemvasia.

~ ~ ~

One of the advantageous side-effects of jet lag is waking, filled with energy, at four in the morning. I reread my guidebook's pages on Monemvasia and, since who knew when next I'd see a laundromat, rinsed the previous day's travelling clothes in the handbasin. After wringing out the sodden fabric as best I could, I draped my laundry around the tiny bathroom – underwear dangling from a rail, leggings suspended from taps, blouse hooked over the soap dish – in the hope it would dry before I had to pack my bags again. There were still hours to fill before the breakfast room opened at nine, so I topped up my water bottle in the colourful Peruvian sling I'd carried around the globe for the last decade and a half. Then I crept out under dark skies to move through narrow lanes, under arches and up and down stairs, my footsteps echoing above the resonant voice of the sea.

A few blocks away, a woman used a garden hose to sluice off the cobblestones in front of a restaurant. *Is she up early? Or is this the end of a long night shift, her last task before she can rest?*

A family of skittish kittens, their supple bodies tangled in play, froze at my approach. Their startled eyes were specks of light at the side of the path.

Apart from those few souls, I was alone. After a precious hour of strolling solitude, I returned to my room for a delicious second sleep before breakfast.

~ ~ ~

It was a steep ascent to the Upper City, where the fortress walls keep watch over the Lower Town and Agia Sofia stands at the edge of a precipice, gazing out at the deep, varying blues of sea and sky. There is one magical spot in this twelfth-century church where a breeze enters through unglazed windows, blessing worshippers and travellers alike with a brief respite of exquisite coolness.

Like its world-renowned namesake – the jewel of Constantinople – Monemvasia's Agia Sofia has been a sacred space for more than one faith. The Ottoman conquerors made it a mosque during both periods of their rule, siting the Turkish hammam next door for ritual cleansing before

Muslim prayers. The bathhouse is now a ruin, sprouting tufts of grass between the stones of its crumbling roof, but the church is a revered place of worship to this day.

After hours of wandering the vestiges of what was once a mighty stronghold, I needed a cold shower, a long drink of water from the fridge and a few minutes in front of an air conditioner. The heat was pulverising. But as I turned to descend, I felt the irresistible tug of an unexplored trail and headed upwards instead. A sweaty trudge took me, as if pulled by a thread, to the broken citadel perched on the highest part of this island nicknamed the Rock. Its two remaining arches jutted from the scrubby ground like inverted keyholes locking giant, invisible doors. They framed views of the causeway and the mainland beyond, where the town of Gefyra climbed to the feet of gentle hills.

On my way back to the hotel, I paused. An intriguing white splodge on the cliff face had caught my eye as I'd hiked up the trail that morning, and now I noticed a pathway leading off in that direction. I couldn't help myself; hot and tired as I was, I *had to* follow that track.

An easy walk led to a short scramble up rough-hewn steps. As I approached, the splodge I'd seen from below resolved into a messy border of white paint outlining the mouth of a cave. A metal door, scored with graffiti, blocked the opening. Behind this ill-fitting barrier nestled a tiny church, its whitewashed interior hung with icons. I couldn't tell whether someone had carved this cavity out of the rockface, or whether it was a natural cave, its edges smoothed by human hands. There were offerings of small-denomination coins laid out in the sign of a cross on an oil-stained tablecloth, and I added my shiniest fifty-cent piece to the collection.

On the path below the cave stood a weatherworn information board. Cracked and peeling, it was so battered by the elements it was almost illegible. I puzzled out what I could: 'A small cave-like church… to the simplest form of hermitage. Fragments of… byzantine… paintings and… graffiti of the name Sveros, with the dates 1713… 764 are preserved in its interior. The Metropolitan… Gabriel… (1539-1618) was a member of the… family from Monemvasia.'

~ ~ ~

By the time I reached my hotel room, it was hot as Hades. *Is Hades hot?* I wondered. *Or am I confusing it with the Christian hell?* The tourist map on the single bedside table showed a swimming area not far away. To get there, I would have to descend to the Portello, the fortified city's southern gate. There might not be any changing facilities, so I'd need to wear my swimsuit under my clothes, just in case.

But, have I mentioned it was hot? Plus, let's face it, my one-piece was not the abbreviated affair I would have sported just five short years earlier. Wearing a bulky bathing costume under my clothing while I explored the town would be uncomfortable. And I didn't relish the idea of clambering back up to my lodgings afterwards, sticky with saltwater, the swimsuit chafing my skin under clammy clothes. It would be worth it if this was my only opportunity to swim in Grecian waters, but I'd soon be heading to Limnisa. This next port of call offered the sweet promise of snorkelling in the placid sea off a private beach, so I decided to give the afternoon swim a miss and made do with taking another shower.

I felt a niggle of guilt for all the showers I was taking to battle the heat, so I kept them brief. Evliya Çelebi, a seventeenth-century Ottoman Turkish travel writer, famously observed of Monemvasia, 'You can find everything you want in this city, except water… one neighbour does not give even a drop of water to the other to drink.' Although the Rock is surrounded by teal-coloured ocean, fresh water has been a treasured resource over the centuries. This was the reason for the enormous, ruined cisterns in the Upper City, waiting through the centuries to catch every ounce of rain that fell from the sky. Thankfully, water is now available from the mainland, and the days when otherwise-generous householders would fiercely guard even a trickle of water have passed.

Reinvigorated by a tall glass of freshly squeezed orange juice that rattled with ice, I set out to discover the picture-postcard village of the Lower Town. This beehive of hotels, homes and churches was unlike anywhere else I'd seen, not least because there wasn't a car in sight or earshot. Although the settlement was pockmarked with the occasional collapsed shell of a building, its character was very different from that of its abandoned Upper City counterpart.

A former mosque houses the town's archaeological collection. It was almost closing time and the man at its door tried to turn me away, but my imploring face overcame the language barrier. He relented, allowing me in for ten minutes. In pride of place in this modest museum stands a marble templon – an architectural screen of sorts – from one of the ruined churches of the Lower Town. Happening across the foundations of this little church a bit later, and imagining where the templon would once have stood, was typical of the simple pleasures of wandering the village.

When I emerged from the museum, a tantalising aroma was playing a silent riff in the air, and I followed the deep herbal notes of this perfume across the square to where it wafted from a thirteenth-century cathedral. The main doors stood shut, just as they had when I'd passed on my pre-dawn ramble, but I peeked in through an open side-entrance. Basil, buckets upon buckets of it, trembled in the breeze from an oscillating electric fan. A woman was gathering up great armfuls of the herb, arranging sheaves of basil where the churches of my childhood would have displayed flowers.

A nineteenth-century lighthouse stood sentinel in the desolate terrain outside the eastern city wall. After the morning's explorations, its copper-coloured lantern appeared the height of modernity, and I soon made my way through an arched portal back into the Lower Town.

Amid the metal sculptures and artfully placed cannonballs in the otherwise empty plaza of Megali Tapia, a plaque was embedded in the stone-paved ground. Trying to decipher its slanted Greek letters, I puzzled out the word 'Geographic' and the name 'Yiannis' before continuing my walk along the southern wall. That's when I spotted the swimming area.

A ladder descended from the edge of the island into the crashing waves. There was a narrow rocky shelf, complete with two intrepid sunbathers, and the booming of the surf hammering against the vast Rock of Monemvasia. That was all.

Thank goodness I'd already decided not to have a swim. If I had come all the way down in my swimsuit, I might have felt obligated to give it a go. And it did *not* look like fun.

~ ~ ~

In the cool refuge of my bedroom, I posted a Facebook photo of the plaque from the empty plaza. It would become the most commented-upon update of my trip.

13 September 2016

Enculturation! I am starting:
1. to be able to read Greek script. Or, at least, sound out the words. In some cases, especially for place names or other words similar to their English equivalents, I could claim this as reading. For example, I'm pretty sure the word in the lower left is something to do with geography.
2. to not loathe olives.
3. to get used to throwing my toilet paper in the bin, not the toilet.

Many of the comments came from online friends I'd made in the glory days of 1990s Yahoo chatrooms, some of whom I'd been lucky enough to meet in person during trips to the United States, England and Spain. Karen, a frequent traveller to the Greek islands, said that when I got home it would take me a while to stop searching for a bin next to the toilet. David, a talented translator who appreciated the quirks of language even more than I did, identified the Greek text. It was an excerpt from the poem 'Geographic Origins' by Yiannis Ritsos. This Nobel Prize-nominated poet was a member of the Greek Resistance during the Second World War, and once described his birthplace as 'My lady Monemvasia, my stone ship'. Bob, Tom and Diana jumped into the olive dispute, and 'real life' friends and family were quick to get involved.

As I pulled the previous day's bottle out of the fridge – all the better to cheer on the debates about olives, linguistics and lavatory paper – it occurred to me that, as a wine from this region, it could well be malmsey.

A snippet of ghoulish trivia: a wine made from local Malvasia grape varietals is the celebrated malmsey in which, according to rumour and Shakespeare's play *Richard III*, George Plantagenet was drowned. Philippa Gregory's version of the tale, in her novel *The White Queen*, has it that King Edward IV granted his treasonous younger brother the royal privilege of choosing the method of his execution. And that's what George chose. *Could this pleasant white be the same wine quaffed by royalty during the War of the Roses?*

It was too hot to want a full meal. Having skipped lunch, though, I needed to track down some kind of supper so as not to wake up hungry at two in the morning. Spurred by my thoughts of malmsey, I headed out on a mission.

Throughout the day, I'd seen hand-painted signboards pointing the way to Byron's Wine Kamara. Hunting for the signs became a game that guided me through the winding lanes between the Portello and the Lower Town's hammam, but when I got to the cellar door, it was closed. Now, I set off to give it another try.

I passed the cathedral and, this time, its doors were flung open, its bright interior adorned with arrangements of fragrant basil. Not wanting to intrude on a religious service, I kept going. The signs led me back to the wine cellar, where Byron himself was sitting at the door, engrossed in a book. After apologising for interrupting, and rather shamefaced at admitting my fascination with the scandalous story, I asked for a glass of malmsey.

As I'd suspected, the wine I drank in my hotel room hadn't been the notorious malmsey at all.

Byron persuaded me first to try a white wine, made from Malvasia grapes but more suited to contemporary palates that have developed to prefer dry wines over sweet. He served it with a light courgette soufflé his wife had baked that afternoon. Then, I had the traditional sweet malmsey dessert wine, *a la* George Plantagenet, Duke of Clarence, with his wife's lemon tart. Byron's wife, not the duke's, of course.

While I sipped and supped, Byron delivered an entertaining history of the wines. malmsey had been an internationally popular tipple from the twelfth century until the fifteenth, but its blend became a lost art when Ottoman Turks occupied the Rock and the nearby mainland. Byron explained the scientific processes winemakers followed at the turn of the twenty-first century to reconstruct the exact blend of sun-dried grape varietals used to create the medieval malmsey.

It was a quiet evening of absorbing conversation. We were soon discussing the ordeals of my workplace, his experiences with mergers and acquisitions in the corporate world before his retirement, and what had happened with municipality amalgamations in Greece. A recent restructure had torn my own work team in Australia apart, upsetting my career and leaving me despondent, but his calm observations were perceptive and encouraging. It was as if he took my arm and guided me a step back from my frustration. With a bit of distance, it was clear that the situation wasn't personal, and that I couldn't control it. If my job was no longer giving me the sense of purpose it once had, that was all the more reason to seek fulfilment elsewhere.

# CHAPTER EIGHT
# MONEMVASIA TO METHANA,
# VIA SPARTA

MY NEXT STOP WOULD be Methana, the almost-island that protrudes like a diamond ring from the thumb of the Peloponnese peninsula. The 7.15 a.m. from Gefyra was the only bus that would get to Corinth Isthmus station in time for my connecting ride. Getting out of Monemvasia early enough to catch it was going to be a challenge.

It was only a couple of kilometres from my hotel room to Gefyra. Even though I needed to leave long before the shuttle started its run, it wasn't the causeway that worried me. It was the first few hundred metres through the village that gave cause for concern. The wheels of my suitcase would struggle, and they'd be far too noisy for that time of the morning. I'd have to carry my luggage over the rough cobblestones but, as you may recall, its main handle had snapped in two on that same path when I arrived. So I was up at five to turn the contents of my bags upside down, stowing the heavy articles in my backpack and the lighter items in the case.

The first part of the walk was as horrible as expected. As quietly as possible, and with frequent pauses to rest my dodgy left arm – a permanent memento of the Sri Lankan bus accident – I lugged my bag across the cobbles to the stone-arched gateway of the Kastro. Then I set the suitcase wheels onto smooth pavement and trundled along the flat road.

I was making better time than anticipated, so I took a break about halfway. Sitting on some handy stone steps at the beginning of a walking trail, I dug into my backpack's side pocket and pulled out my breakfast, unwrapping the sandwiches which the obliging hotel staff had parcelled up the previous night. As a pink haze grew in the east, I munched appreciatively through bread and cheese, a little disappointed not to find any olives.

After packing the last sandwich away for later, I continued around the Rock, along the causeway and over a bridge I hadn't noticed when we'd sped across by car a couple of days earlier. A small sign explained that this had been yet another level of defence. Until the late nineteenth century, 'there stood a construction with fourteen arches and a wooden drawbridge in the middle, which was hauled up in the event of enemy attack.'

I arrived at the bus station early, so I stood outside its deserted office and took picture after fuzzy picture of the Rock in the poor light before putting my phone away to save its battery. An elderly man crossed the bridge towards me, calling and gesticulating. I never found out what he was so insistent on communicating; after a dozen shrugs and baffled looks on my part, he threw up his hands in exasperation and wandered away.

The office opened as the bus pulled in, just in time for me to buy my ticket. This scrap of paper would take me as far as Corinth Isthmus, but what was I going to do during the five-hour wait there for my connecting bus? There'd be some way to get the eight kilometres from the transit station to the city, and then on to the archaeological complex of Ancient Corinth, but what if I couldn't make it back for the last bus to Limnisa? Plus, I'd have my clumsy luggage to manage. My travel instincts rebelled at wasting this time when the heritage sites would be so enticingly within reach, but anxiety was already tightening around my throat.

This was a problem for later. For now, I took my ticket and the information that I would need to change buses in Sparta, and settled down to enjoy the ride as best I could. As we pulled away, I glanced over my shoulder. The rising sun was a fiery ball in the sky behind the shadowed Rock.

~ ~ ~

Just as on the trip from Athens, the bus ride between Monemvasia and Sparta meandered through picturesque villages and landscapes. This time, we picked up dozens of teenaged school kids along the way. Whenever we passed a church, the girls' fingers would dance through the Greek Orthodox triple sign of the cross, while their giggling chatter continued, uninterrupted.

Sparta presented an unexpected bonus. The driver announced that there would be a brief wait at the bus station, enough for a bathroom break. Pausing at the enquiry desk, I found I could halt my journey there for three hours, with the next scheduled bus able to get me to Corinth Isthmus in plenty of time to make my connection. Even better, I could leave my bags in an unlocked luggage room, at no charge, though at my own risk.

I'd known of Sparta for decades, of course, having first encountered its warriors in my childhood reading of *Asterix at the Olympic Games*. But this was an unplanned stop, and I didn't have my bearings in the modern city. The bus station was a bit outside the town centre, but, after puzzling over the tiny map in my guidebook, I chanced a lucky guess and headed in the right direction.

A brisk walk took me past a fire station, where I snapped a few photos of the trucks for my partner Adam – an Aussie firefighter – and then to a plaza in front of a church. Although it was a Wednesday morning, people were pouring out through the timber doors and gathering in the cafés that lined the square. They were all clutching sprays of basil.

It turned out the bounteous basil marked a religious feast day. On 14 September, Greek Orthodox churches celebrate the Elevation of the Holy Cross, commemorating the discovery of this relic by the first Christian Roman empress. Her name was Augusta Imperatrix Flavia Julia Helena, but my Catholic parents might have known her as Saint Helen. She was the mother of Constantine the Great, the man credited with founding Constantinople.

My mother hardly ever spoke with me about her travels, but I once overheard her talking about the time she ditched her group and headed out for a solo meal. Of all the far more important life lessons she tried to instil, the one that stuck was to 'eat where the locals eat.' Bypassing an airy café with plenty of empty seats on its terrace, I made for the busiest establishment and weaved my way into its depths, through a labyrinth of crowded tables obscured by billowing cigarette smoke.

Ancient Sparta was infamous for its unpalatable cuisine, with one long-ago visitor remarking, after tasting their broth made from pig's blood and vinegar, that at last he understood why Spartan warriors weren't afraid to die. Taking a more optimistic approach, I ordered a small serving of sliced sausages seasoned with oranges and a glass of fresh juice. While waiting for the food, I read up on what I could see during this unexpected Spartan respite.

It seemed that, despite being one of the best-known civilisations of Ancient Greece, Sparta chose to expend its riches on winning wars rather than on constructing monumental buildings. The guidebook warned that the remains of Sparta weren't as spectacular as many other sites but mentioned that visiting the northern end of town would be worthwhile. And, indeed, it was.

An impressive statue of King Leonidas guarded the way to the archaeological sites, with the legendary quote, '*Molon Labe*' ('Come and get them') inscribed at his feet. These are the words attributed to a vastly outnumbered Leonidas at the Battle of Thermopylae in 480 BCE, when the Persian king Xerxes demanded that he and his three hundred Spartans lay down their weapons. The phrase has been immortalised in popular culture, from Plutarch's writings in antiquity to Hollywood movies made in 1962 and 2007. Seeing the words made me smile, recalling the passion with which Dimitri had related the tale of this battle during our walking tour in Athens.

Except for a group of five I spotted in the distance, I had the acropolis to myself, but I had to watch the clock to make sure I wouldn't miss the bus. It was a whirlwind excursion, but I was able to admire the magnificent outlook over the city to the serried ranks of the Taÿgetos Mountains, sit on marble seats in the crumbling theatre set into a green hillside, and peer down into the excavated agora, Sparta's marketplace of old. Byzantine ruins sat among the Roman and Ancient Greek remains and, as I followed the ghosts of bygone priests through a semi-circular ambulatory behind a tumbledown church, I felt a haunting connection with the seventh century.

My spirits were high as I collected my luggage and boarded the bus. I hadn't considered that my allocated seating was on the earlier coach, which had long since driven away. This bus didn't even *have* a Seat Twenty, but there was a spare place for me, and I travelled on without incident.

~ ~ ~

The first thing I did on arriving at Corinth Isthmus station was buy my onward ticket. Of all my bus, train, plane and boat rides while in Greece, this was the one about which I felt the most uneasy. My other trips were to definite destinations, often the last stop or at least a major junction. Now, though, I was travelling to Limnisa, a writers' retreat some kilometres outside a small village named Agios Georgios. There was a larger town, Methana, about twenty minutes' drive from there, but even Methana wasn't on the bus route. I'd need to ask the driver to let me off at Agios Apostoli where, my hosts had promised, a taxi would be waiting to meet me.

The woman at the desk took my money and handed me a ticket in exchange. She rattled off some complicated instructions, which I couldn't understand at all. She tried again. Feeling inadequate, I nodded through my confusion, said, '*Efcharistó*,' and decided to ask again closer to the departure time. I had more than two hours to hope an English-speaking official might come on duty.

There's not much to do near the bus station of Corinth Isthmus, apart from taking a short walk to inspect the channel separating the Peloponnese peninsula from the Greek mainland. This is the famed Corinth Canal that had passed in a breathtaking blur as our coach crossed over a few days before. Both a feature of majestic beauty and a harrowing scar on the landscape, its scale is humbling even as it fills you with pride in the endeavours of humankind. And there's a good chance that the awe it inspires may fizzle into clouds of vertigo when you peer over the precipice.

The earliest plans for the canal date back more than two thousand years, but it wasn't completed until the nineteenth century. Stretching a little over six kilometres from the Gulf of Corinth to the Saronic Gulf, it is a V-shaped gash cut through almost a hundred near-vertical metres of dirt and striated rock. At its widest point, it's only about twenty-five metres across the water's surface.

A narrow pedestrian bridge, adjacent to the road, spans the canal. My intent was to stroll to the mainland and back, but it took only a few steps onto the walkway, which shuddered with the motion of passing traffic, to rouse my acrophobia. The Greek *akro* that tells us the *Acro*polis stands on a high hilltop means 'peak'. It also means 'edge' and my *acro*phobic fear of heights is more about how close I am to the brink than it is about my altitude.

Now, I wasn't just near the edge, I was over it.

The rockface plunged down in bands of ever paler shades, from ochre at the top, approaching white before losing all colour in its own shadow at the base, and then disappearing into murky water far, far below. I snapped a series of shaky photos, then made a hasty retreat to the bus station where I had, after all, left my suitcase unattended.

There was a café inside, and a comfortable waiting area. There were also half a dozen scruffy dogs, apparently strays, lounging around the low benches outside. One of these was suffering from a shocking case of mastitis. Her entire under-torso was engorged, with swollen teats, and streaks of blood and pus visible under the taut skin. I couldn't think what to do for her except to give her some nutrition.

The café didn't sell much that was suitable for animals, but I selected a couple of sausage rolls we could share. I had no idea whether pastry was bad for dogs, so I peeled off the flaky filo and ate it myself, giving her the meaty filling. She was pleased with the arrangement, thumping her tail on the ground and following me to the waiting room afterwards, though she stopped at the door. She knew she wasn't allowed inside.

I sat for a while, trying to focus on my book instead of fretting about the dog, but I couldn't stop worrying about her. So I dug out my padlock keys, opened my suitcase and rummaged through my underwear, now on display for everyone around me. Locating my first-aid kit, I pulled out the spray-on antiseptic. Out I trudged to treat the dog's belly, much to the surprise of the other travellers.

She didn't like the spray as much as she'd enjoyed the sausage. This antiseptic didn't sting, but her inflamed skin may have been so sensitive that even the cool spray caused her pain. She glared at me in reproach as she heaved herself up from her spot under a bench and lumbered away.

The antiseptic wouldn't do much to heal the infection – she needed a full course of antibiotics – but it was distressing to accept there was nothing I could do for her. At home, I would have known where to take her for help. Here, I was powerless.

~ ~ ~

Corinth Isthmus is a busy station, with scores of buses passing through as their fat tyres take them all over the Peloponnese and onto the mainland. As the time for my departure neared, my anxiety grew. My stop was Agios Apostoli, but I'd forgotten the bus's final destination, so couldn't search the Greek letters on the windscreen signs for clues to which coach I should board. Plus, there were no numbered bays here. Coaches simply pulled in at the empty patch in front of the building, stopped for a few moments, and then drove off again. The same lady at the ticket counter could only give the same incomprehensible instructions as before, and the few people I approached didn't have much English.

A young woman overheard my awkward queries and came to my aid. Her bus would leave before mine was due to arrive, but she dashed inside, checked the name of my bus's last stop and returned to write 'Galatas' on my ticket in both Greek and English script. She waved away my thanks with a grin as her own ride pulled up and she climbed aboard.

I tucked the ticket into my phrase book on the page starting, in phonetically spelled-out syllables, with: 'Pa-ra-ka-*lo pe*-ste mu *o*-tan *fta*-su-me sti…' This phrase (Please tell me when we get to…) seemed an impossible challenge, and, despite my best intentions, I chickened out of trying it out loud. Instead, I relied on a pitiful attempt at 'Agios Apostoli' with a pleading expression on my face.

This didn't work so well with the driver. He gave a brusque nod, but, when our vehicle stopped alongside another parked near a sign for the Ancient Theatre of Epidavros, it was a kind-hearted fellow passenger who let me know I needed to change buses. I scrambled out, barely in time to pull my suitcase from the luggage compartment, and got into the new bus. This driver was friendlier and called me when we arrived at my stop.

My taxi was waiting. Its driver, Nikos, was a sociable chap well-accustomed to ferrying foreigners to and from Limnisa. He was keen to chat. In Greek, naturally.

After I'd told him how I was and where I came from – I think that's what he was asking – there wasn't much more we could discuss to pass the half-hour journey. He pointed out the smelly sulphur baths in Methana and the three islands of Poros, Aegina, and Agistri. A dutiful student, I repeated the names back to him. There were some structures in the water that looked like the oyster farms I see on my occasional commute to Sydney, so I asked him, with one word and a gesture, if they were for *thalassina* (seafood). He replied that no, they were for *psari* (fish). Despite his valiant efforts at conversation, all the rest, as Shakespeare wrote, 'was Greek to me'. I resolved to master a few phrases for my return trip in a week's time.

# CHAPTER NINE
## METHANA MEDITATIONS

**B**Y THE TIME THE taxi pulled over at the side of the dark road outside Limnisa, I'd been travelling for more than fifteen hours, including four bus rides. Nikos opened the boot to get my suitcase. When he saw the broken handle, I learned a new Greek word, *provlima*. This means exactly what it sounds like: a problem.

The house wasn't visible from the road, but Nikos helped me and my problematic suitcase two-thirds of the way along the pebbled path, then left me in sight of the cheerful lights around the outdoor dining area. The household had just sat down at the table, where an American with smiling eyes was about to share a verse he'd written for his wife's birthday. 'God danced on the day you were born,' Bill toasted Denise with the lyrical elegance of a poet.

Soon I was eating, drinking and chatting with a fascinating group of writers. I was also feeling like something of a fraud.

~ ~ ~

You see, when I started planning this expedition to Greece, I knew little about the country. I needed a hook, something meaningful around which to construct my itinerary. Given the profound impact of our yoga tour through northern India six months before – the journey that became the catalyst I needed to tackle my fear of road travel in general and buses in particular – I began by researching yoga retreats in Greece.

The internet turned up page after page of results. Many were exorbitantly priced, but there were a few affordable alternatives. Without even an inkling of which parts of Greece to visit, though, the abundance of choice was paralysing. Then, scrolling through myriad listings, I had a *Eureka!* moment. My keyword search for 'yoga retreat Greece' had turned up something unexpected.

Limnisa is not a yoga *shala*. It is a writers' retreat: a home lined with books and a garden – filled with terraces and hammocks and writing nooks in surprising places – that leads down to the wide blue waters of the Saronic Gulf. Writers travel to Limnisa for its tranquil working environment, literary conversations over home-cooked vegetarian fare, and guidance from Mariel and Philip, authors themselves, who run the retreat.

There is also an optional group yoga practice each morning, which triggered the search engine hit.

Now, in case I have given the impression that I'm an advanced yogi, let me disillusion you. I am a vibrant young adventurer living in the body of a plump, middle-aged woman who doesn't exercise as often as she should. I recently came across a meme on social media that struck a chord. It quoted a romance author named S.L. Jennings: 'In my mind, I am this awesome adventurous badass. But in reality, I am just a bookworm that really likes wine.'

I enjoy yoga, but I'm not particularly consistent, accomplished, fit or strong. In fact, I am the exact opposite of every graceful yogi I've ever admired. When people ask why I don't drive, I sometimes counter with, 'Have you seen me walk?' I'm clumsy and uncoordinated, with poor spatial awareness. My arms and legs are an ever-changing display of bruises from walking into doorknobs, bumping into furniture or tripping over nothing at all, scattering lost property as I go.

A Greek yoga retreat would be blissful, but I wasn't wedded to the plan. And I fell in love with Limnisa through its website. It is far from the tourist areas, and it took a couple of tries before I could locate it on Google maps. It's within walking distance of a village with no shops or banks or bustle, although there are two taverns, and the baker visits almost every day. Mornings at the retreat go by in an industrious hush as everyone settles to their work. At lunchtime, the mandatory silence ends. You can spend the afternoon walking, swimming, snorkelling, cycling, napping, reading or chatting. Or continuing to write, if you so wish.

The *provlima*? I wasn't a writer.

This book wasn't even a glimmer in my mind until well after my return to Australia. Granted, I have always been interested in words and had fun shaping them. I had written some short pieces a decade or more before, and I'd been lucky to have a handful of them published, but I was more casual hobbyist than dedicated wordsmith. In recent years, my writing had been limited to compiling corporate business cases and briefing notes.

But Limnisa called to me. Stress had been building throughout my workplace, spreading into every aspect of my existence. The tension was encroaching on the hours that I should have devoted to my home, my family, even my sleep. I was desperate for a chance to take stock and work out what I wanted from the life that was slipping away from me, second by second, month by month. The notion of slowing down for a whole week – to rest and dine on healthy meals prepared by caring hands, and to do so in the company of creative writers – utterly seduced me.

I sent a tentative email, explaining that, instead of writing, I hoped to use my time at the retreat for 'walking and reading and just thinking. I am in great need of time to mull.'

Mariel replied: 'Writing, walking, reading, thinking and mulling is what we all do at Limnisa. You are very welcome to stay with us.' She encouraged me to have a project of some kind to occupy the silent mornings of the retreat. Beyond that, there were no expectations.

Limnisa had no one room available for the duration of my stay, so Mariel and I patched together a sequence of two bedrooms and a garden tent to cover my travel dates, and she helped me navigate the complex public transport timetabling required to make my itinerary work. Meanwhile, I fussed over what my 'project' should be. I toyed with an idea for a children's book, but the thought of dragging my heavy old laptop computer around Greece was daunting, and I've never found it easy to write longhand in notebooks or peck away at a touchscreen tablet. I didn't underestimate my goal to retreat from the demands of day-to-day obligations and assess what mattered, but I couldn't see myself tackling this as a structured project with designated pondering time between 8.30 a.m. and 1.15 p.m.

Then it came to me. Whenever I travel to a new country, I try to learn a bit of the language. This time, when I opened my new phrase book, the words for 'please', 'thank you', 'good morning', and 'good evening' were familiar. They'd been lurking in my subconscious since a long-forgotten flirtation with a Greek waiter, on a five-day cruise along the Mozambican coast with my brother's wife, Fiona, back in 2003.

I didn't have the mental space to stockpile more phrases in the mad rush to get everything ready before my flight, so I downloaded a dozen free 'teach yourself Greek' apps onto Adam's iPad and packed it, with some earphones, for a week's silent study. That would be my project.

~ ~ ~

Now, here I was, seated at Limnisa's dinner table, and it felt as if I were breaking bread with the demigods. Authors, to me, were mythical beings who filled my hours, weeks, months and years with multitudes of stories. They had populated my imagination with thousands of literary characters since my childhood, yet here they were, in animated conversation about the writing challenges they'd faced that day. These people had created such books, such characters. They were creating them in their minds even as we spoke.

I was enthralled.

I had stepped into an extraordinary community, and even though one or two faces around the table changed each night, the sense of kinship was sustained throughout the week. The writers were a varied bunch, hailing from Germany, England, Australia, the Netherlands and the United States of America. Many of them lived in countries not of their birth and spoke multiple languages. Between them, they were working on novels, plays, screenplays, short stories, children's books, sermons and academic texts. Some drew or painted or wrote poetry when taking breaks from their main projects. The only other person who hadn't come to Limnisa to write was a journalist. Like me, she was going through stressful changes at work as she moved from one role to another. Unlike me, her project for the week was a complicated knitting pattern.

Breakfasts were solitary, a buffet of bread and butter, rich honey and shavings from a hunk of a hard sheep's cheese called *graviera*, creamy yoghurt and a medley of fruit salad. Lunches and dinners were colourful concoctions of fresh local produce including *horta*, strong-tasting wild mountain greens that featured in the books I'd been reading. The writers took their midday meals whenever their appetites happened to distract them from their muses, but evenings brought the entire Limnisa family together in a feast of humour and the shared love of language.

Dinner conversation was an eye-opener. Somehow, I had always assumed authors knew at least the broad strokes of their plots before they sat down to write. The notion of characters and even the story itself developing organically during the writing process had never occurred to me. I have long admired creators of fiction, who construct coherent stories from infinite possibilities, but this new revelation – that someone could type the first lines of a novel with no idea of how it might end – was mesmerising.

The retreat provided a routine rather than a program, and a highlight of this routine was the much-anticipated daily appearance of a freshly baked cake at 4.00 p.m. The spirited dinner conversations continued, though more sedately, over afternoon tea. They even followed us into the sea, where we discussed imagery and voice and character – and speculated on the flavour of cake the next day would bring – as we floated in groups of three or four in warm, silky water. And, always, there was the opportunity to retire to a secluded space to read or nap or simply bask in the pleasure of being alone.

~ ~ ~

In many ways, my week at Limnisa was the most uneventful of my travels, a hiatus from adventure. In others, it was the most significant. It had a deep effect on my psyche – deep enough to inspire a dream, weeks later, in which I was writing this book.

My memories of the retreat are a series of sensory vignettes:

A meditative communal mini hike in the quiet of evening, through olive groves and pomegranate orchards.

In contrast, hurrying around with the rest of the group, laughing as we gathered up cushions and rugs in advance of a coming storm. The weather made the sky broody and turned the crystal waters mysteriously dark and choppy.

Swotting over several language apps while lounging on the cushions of a bench built into the veranda wall. They taught me basic niceties and lists of colours, numbers, animals and foods. I rehearsed the most useful phrases: 'I'm sorry, I don't understand,' and how to order a glass of wine. What the apps didn't teach me is that, in this part of Greece, it is more common to order wine by the quarter – or half-kilo (or litre), rather than by the glass. Luckily, Mariel was there to fill this knowledge gap: all I had to do was substitute the word *tetarto* (quarter) for *potiri* (glass), and I was good to go.

Taking a solo walk to the village of Agios Georgios, visiting the church to see its icons of Saint George slaying the dragon, then sitting at the harbourside taverna and nursing a *tetarto* of white wine with a bowl of ice cubes on the side, all ordered in my stumbling Greek.

My first room-hop, from an upstairs sea-view room to a tent in the garden, just steps from the small pebble beach. The tent was comfortable enough, but, in deep summer, it was a trifle warm for my taste. On our host Philip's suggestion, I hung a mosquito net over the cushioned veranda bench I had claimed as my daytime study nook. This created a breezy bower where I spent the next two nights, falling asleep to the lapping of gentle water against the shore.

The luxury of paperbacks, as opposed to my e-reader. I raced through three books, all set in Greece, from Limnisa's well-populated shelves. It was a surreal moment when, partway through the second, *Acropolis: Curse of Athena*, I noticed Philip's name on the cover.

Grappling with conflicting emotions: sometimes luxuriating in the enforced restfulness, at other times beating my head against an unexpected guilt. I was halfway across the world in Greece. How dare I not be out exploring, doing, experiencing with every available minute?

My embarrassment towards the end of my stay when I had to confess to Mariel that I'd broken what I had presumed was a luggage stand. Her magazine rack had bravely supported my suitcase for days before collapsing in a splintered heap.

Reading 'Iced Tea', the winning entry in Limnisa's short story competition. First prize in this annual writing contest was a week's residence at the retreat, and the 2016 winner's stay overlapped with mine. Kathryn was a young Aussie who was living in Britain at the time, and she wrote with a gut-wrenching power that tapped into the troubling thoughts I was having about my mother. I made a note to watch for Kathryn's work and was elated when her debut novel, *Hitch*, later won Penguin Random House Australia's literary prize. That's Kathryn Hind. I wish I could say you'd heard her name from me first.

And the hours spent leafing through Mum's diary, searching for that elusive sense of connection. These pages should have been bringing us closer, but she was still a stranger to me. I couldn't remember a time when we'd known how to talk to each other. It was as if I were a child shaking a snow globe. My emotions would swirl and rise and swirl again, but they always settled in the same place: a single memory from the 1980s, during the most turbulent of my teenage years.

You'd think I'd have fixated on the more dramatic memories. One of the times I ran away from the claustrophobia of our suburban family home, say. Or that awful day a supermarket security guard caught me shoplifting, just young enough, at thirteen, to escape prosecution. Maybe the occasion of my mother calling the cops because she thought she'd found marijuana in my tip of a bedroom (the evidence turned out to be shrivelled mandarin peels at the bottom of my wastepaper bin). Or the painful months after I broke the news I wouldn't join in the sacrament of confirmation with my Catholic schoolmates. But, while those clashes of wills might make for better storytelling, my regrets converged on a much more mundane moment.

Arriving home from school, I'd found my mother waiting in a state of anxiety. She had tried to bleach a slight stain from my favourite shirt, one of the few on-trend fashion items I owned, and the chemical had left an ugly purple mark on the white fabric. She'd clearly been dreading breaking this news to me all day.

Her stumbling apologies gave me a terrible pang. I'd had that hollowed-out feeling – of having disappointed someone, of having messed up – often enough myself. But I was mired in inarticulate adolescence. I couldn't find the words to reassure her that I understood she was trying to do something nice for me, that I wouldn't be angry for damage born from good intentions.

At the backyard clothesline, we discovered the purple had faded to nothing, as if by magic, as the garment had dried in the sunshine. All was well.

Except it wasn't. That my mother had been so afraid of my reaction shamed me, but I was incapable of reaching out to her beyond a shrugged, 'It's okay, Mum.'

We never spoke of it again. I didn't know how to tell her that I hadn't wanted to cause her pain, and now I never can. As I grew from a wayward adolescent to a determined young woman with a very different moral compass from that of my parents, the gap between us widened. If only she had lived a little longer, we might have bridged that void.

~ ~ ~

On my last evening at Limnisa, as we sat around the dinner table, someone admired the outdoor pizza oven and commented that we'd eaten no pizza during our stay. They had just built it, explained Philip and Mariel, and it was not yet ready for baking. Later, someone else asked if Limnisa had any 'skeletons in its closet.' The banter devolved into hilarity, with much speculation as to the real function of the oven as a receptacle for unexplained bodies, and about how guests supposedly left in the pre-dawn darkness for the '6.30 a.m.

ferry' (insert crooked finger air quotes here), never to be seen again.

Sadly, it was my turn to disappear into the night. I left the group laughing over wine and dessert, to get ready for my departure before the sun came up.

# CHAPTER TEN
# METHANA TO METEORA

NIKOS WAS DUE TO pick me up at 5.50 a.m., so I was
up before daybreak to throw the last few things
into my bags, sneak out of the slumbering house,
and haul my problematic luggage up the pebbled path.

Although my Greek vocabulary had increased a hundredfold
in the past week, my aspiration of chatting with Nikos on
this return drive was unrealistic. Numbers and colours will
take you only so far, and lists of animals, family members
and foodstuffs, not much further. Nevertheless, he escorted
me to buy my ferry ticket from a tiny shop stocked with
newspapers and cigarettes, the single point of light amid the
shuttered businesses lining Methana's main street. Then we
drove to the deserted wharf, where we shared an awkward
silence until the boat arrived.

The boat's noisy indoor lounge was stale and stuffy, so I
made for the outside deck where, still groggy from the anti-
seasickness medication I'd taken the night before, I passed the

two-hour commute in a sleepy huddle. Sunrise stretched her rosy fingers across the chilly heavens, gathering her strength to stoke the furnace for another hot day.

Our stop to pick up passengers from Aegina was an unexpected blessing. This island, with its whitewashed wharf-side chapel and lone Grecian pillar stabbing up at the sky from the promontory adjacent to the harbour, was one of three my mother had visited four decades earlier. With my own fingers made clumsy by the cold, I consulted her diary:

> … Bus to boat SARONIC STAR at 8. Set out for glorious day at Greek islands. Rainy, but Father + I stayed on deck. Went walking on Aegina. Chased Hen. Talked about Modesty Blaise + BARON + other books with Father who bought blue sailor cap… Ate John's grapes on deck. Off to Poros. Paddled in puddles & took photos. Back to boat. Father bombed by gull. Onto Hydra. Wandered through streets with Mom Father & Johnny. Donkey tied to tree. All houses closed. Drank beer. Thousands of cats. Walked up to cannons. Climbed down steps to sea. Back to boat at 4 & off once more. Docked & home by bus in dark. Bought wine on boat & we all had sandwiches in my room.

My mother's record of the islands didn't convey anything of their history or culture; she seemed more taken with Father Martin, the Catholic priest leading their pilgrimage. Our approaches to travel couldn't have been more different.

But perhaps there were a few similarities, when I came to think about it. Her notes overflowed with references to conversations and personal relationships, humble food memories, book discussions and inside jokes. There was even a mention of finding the little diary in Jerusalem's Holy Sepulchre after she'd dropped it there six days before. She credited this mini miracle to Saint Anthony, the patron saint of lost things, whereas I attribute my frequent finds of mislaid belongings to good luck. Plus, Mum's islands were overrun with animals: volatile seagulls and persecuted chickens, captive donkeys, and sprawling cats lording it over them all.

But I had to take her word for that. Although I admired them from a distance, I wouldn't be setting foot on any of these islands during this trip. She flew out of Athens the morning after her island tour, and this fragile link to the woman she had been – when she wasn't being my mum – ended with the turn of a handwritten page.

At least, I thought it did.

~ ~ ~

I arrived in the port of Piraeus in good cheer, unaware that this day was to be one of only two negative experiences during my travels in Greece.

When purchasing my train ticket to Meteora weeks before, my finger had hovered over the payment button while I fought with indecision. The railways in Greece aren't as popular as the intercity bus networks, and they have a reputation for being less reliable. Although it was a relief not to be boarding yet another bus, who could say whether the trains would be running on schedule? Greek public transport systems are prone to work stoppages, and recent arrivals at Limnisa had said there'd been a strike earlier in the week. As far as I knew, though, the trains were back on track.

The five-hour rail journey would be a welcome respite from all the road travel and the anxiety that gripped me each time I got onto a bus. I just had to find the Metro to Omonia. There, I'd change lines for Larissa Station, where I could relax until my train pulled in. I was an old hand at the Athens Metro by now – I'd ridden the underground twice and emerged at my intended destination both times. Although I wasn't sure how to get to Piraeus Station, how hard could it be? For once, I wasn't stressed. I had hours to spare, and an A-class ticket from Larissa Station to Meteora's Kalambaka Station in my pocket. After all, it's not often you can travel first class for only a few extra euros.

Ferry passengers funnelled through the gate in the harbour's fence, running the gauntlet of taxi drivers seeking fares. One called out in English to ask where I was going. When I said I was looking for the Metro, he pointed the way with a good-natured smile.

'But,' he said, 'there is a Metro strike today. Some of the trains are not running. What train do you want?'

'I need to get to Omonia.'

He gave an easy shrug. 'Well, if you don't want my taxi, don't go with the Metro. Go with the bus, number forty-nine.' He gestured in the direction of the bus stop.

Appreciating that he was taking time to help me when he had nothing to gain from the transaction, I explained I'd be heading on from Omonia to Larissa Station and asked if he knew the number of a bus going there. He didn't. 'Maybe someone will tell you at the bus stop. Or go to Omonia and then you ask.'

I bid him a grateful '*Adio*' and trundled past the line of taxis. I hadn't gone fifty paces when I stopped and reassessed. I'd counted on today being bus-free. Being forced into one felt unfair. My trip was more than halfway through, and I'd done well with my budget. I could afford to splurge on an inessential taxi ride, this once, for the sake of a hassle-free commute. And this was a nice man; I wanted to support his business.

I turned back to the friendly driver, we agreed on a fare, and I climbed into the front seat. As he battled the morning traffic, he told me about his father, a sailor who had visited South Africa many years before. We talked about his children, two young girls. When he explained that I was his last fare before he headed home, I said that Adam often worked nights, too. Soon, we were comparing notes on the pros and cons of the shift-working life. He dropped me off outside the train station more than four hours before my train was due to leave, and I gave him an extravagant tip.

You're supposed to check in large luggage for a small fee – although I later discovered this is more a guideline than a rule, with many people muscling their bulky belongings into the passenger compartments. When I tried to hand in my bag, the man staffing the luggage office pointed at a clock on the wall, miming that it was far too early. With a broad grin, he swung himself over the counter by one hand, grabbed my suitcase and led me to a wall of lockers. For a couple of euros, I could free myself from my baggage for an unexpected expedition into the city.

Venturing underground to check the transportation situation, I was thankful to find there were Metro trains running from here. I'd visited all my personal must-sees in Athens, and then some, but there was so much else to explore. Going too far afield might put my onward travel plans at risk, though, so I opted for a morning at the museum. It was only ten minutes' walk from Victoria Station, and it would give me an unanticipated bonus: one last Greek touchpoint with Mum.

At least, I thought it would be the last.

The National Archaeological Museum is notable for the quality of its collection, not its modernity or innovative displays. It houses old-school exhibitions, its halls lined with glass cabinets or filled with statues on plinths. Nevertheless, visitors flock to such treasures as the Mask of Agamemnon, an impressive golden death mask from Mycenae showing a man with a prissy little moustache. It was disappointing to learn that, despite its name, there's not much chance the mask belonged to Helen of Troy's vengeful brother-in-law.

Mum recorded that she saw 'Horse + boy, Poseidon, Jewelry' and I could see why these artefacts made an impression on her. The most striking was the second-century BCE *Jockey of Artemision*. Archaeologists pieced this life-sized bronze together after it had lain for centuries shipwrecked and broken on the ocean floor. The child jockey's facial expression was unsettling in its intensity as he hunched over his mount, urging it forward. It didn't take much imagination to hear the thudding of hooves, feel the animal's muscles bunching under the boy's thighs as – nostrils flaring – it leapt into the unknown. It was all I could do not to reach out and wipe away the invisible foam that flecked the creature's mouth.

Another treat awaited in the upper-storey gallery: frescoes from Akrotiri, a seventeenth-century BCE archaeological site on Santorini, where I would be visiting in a few days.

I admired the wall paintings that had been transported to the capital, including the famous mural known as *The Boxing Boys*, but I was feeling the press of time to return to Larissa Station, concerned that I couldn't rely on the Metro running to schedule. And, to be frank, there were pressing messages coming from my bladder as well. It was time to leave the museum's majestic halls and return to the mundanity of present-day reality and its calls of nature.

At least I hadn't encountered the 'Man with whistle' mentioned in Mum's journal. But that might be because I was better behaved. I hadn't 'Joked about Archimedes' or 'Looked up at leg' either. I'll never know whose leg that was, but in my mind it was the formidable bronze Poseidon with the washboard abs who endured the indignities of this gawking group. The 'Martini + Roll' my usually moderate mum had for lunch might have had something to do with it, but it was still baffling. *Who is this woman, and what has she done with my mother? I don't recognise her at all.*

I wanted more from Mum's Greek travel jottings than these seven tiny pages could give.

~ ~ ~

After a quick bathroom break and an impulsive stop at a supermarket, I made my way to the Metro. And this was where the day began to sour.

Within a couple of minutes, I was speeding to Larissa Station, once again unaffected by the Metro strike, and beginning to wonder whether the affable taxi driver had taken me for more than one ride. Had there even been a strike, or was that just a hustle to get me into his cab? Had the pleasant, helpful man with whom I'd spent half an hour chatting that morning been manipulating me the entire time? The suspicion settled like lead in my stomach as I arrived at the station, retrieved my luggage and checked it in. *Am I so out of travelling practice that I've fallen for a blatant tourist scam?* I liked to pretend I was a savvy traveller, but I'd been a complete fool.

There was an hour before the train would arrive, and it was as good a time as any to make my single planned ATM withdrawal: the five hundred euros I needed for the rest of my holiday.

I avoid using bank machines when travelling, if I can. The last thing I need is to have an ATM swallow my card. If I do need cash, I try to use a machine attached to a branch. That way, if something goes wrong, there are staff who can help. And yet, even as these considerations crossed my mind, I broke with my usual practice. At the ATM embedded in the station wall, I selected the option for English text, inserted my card, keyed in the PIN and took care to study each screen of instructions. A final click of a silver button completed the transaction. The machine buzzed and spat out the card.

That was it. No banknotes. No explanation. Just the standard welcome message, which was no bloody help at all, blinking at me.

I searched the machine with frantic fingers, but everything was sealed tight. I couldn't even identify which slot was supposed to issue the cash. I didn't know the phone number for the bank, had no means to call – without a local SIM card, my device was not much more than a camera – and wouldn't have been able to communicate my problem even if I had. A telephone call that would have been a tedious chore at home, in English, was an insurmountable task here.

I turned away from the machine, then hurried back to double-check. There was nothing to indicate any transaction had ever happened. I rushed to the information counter inside the station. There, the man at the desk informed me, his deep voice doleful, 'I know trains, not banks.'

Helpless to resolve the situation, I paced the dreary waiting room. My stomach, already empty, was now twisting with anxiety. In the station café, I bought a mediocre sausage roll, which sat like cardboard on my tongue and concrete in my belly, joining the lead weight I'd been carrying since I first suspected a taxi rip-off. Had I just lost five hundred euros?

I told myself to let it go, not to take the taxi scam to heart, not to agonise about the money. The taxi driver had provided a convenient commute in exchange for his fare, even if he did trick me out of the cheaper Metro alternative, and he probably needed the cash more than I did. *As for the unsuccessful withdrawal*, I thought, *if the money's gone, it's gone.* While it would be a massive blow to my budget, I was privileged to be in a position where I wouldn't go hungry because of it.

The thing with anxiety, though, is that you can't always rationalise it away.

When the train arrived, I located my window seat in a comfortable compartment with four other women and a young girl. I tried to lose myself in the scenery and the rhythm of the train, but I was stewing in self-pity.

The first hour dragged on forever. Then the girl's mother asked if she could plug her phone into the USB port next to my seat, and we started to chat. I soon knew a little of each traveller's story. The young mother and her well-behaved child were Greek and were travelling home from a stay in the city. The single, older woman was also Greek, but devoted half of each year to living with her daughter in the United States. The other two were Americans, a mother and her adult daughter who, like me, were travelling to Meteora.

While the remainder of the trip was still a quiet one, with the five adults reading, napping or watching the world pass by outside the windows, the carriage became a friendlier space. After a while, I plucked up the nerve to find out whether my misgivings were justified.

'Was there a Metro strike this morning?'

'No, nothing like that. The Athens Metro was running as usual.'

It wasn't the answer I wanted, but at least now I could stop fretting about it. Next, I asked about the ATM.

'Maybe the machine ran out of money?' guessed one of the Greek travellers.

'That happens sometimes,' agreed the other.

They sensed my anxiety about the missing cash, I think, but they did their best to distract me with questions about where I'd been so far in Greece and where I planned to visit. When I told them I had a hankering for a meaty dinner after a week of wholesome vegetarianism, the young mother recommended the *païdakia*, which she translated as 'the small ribs of the lamb', in a taverna in Kastraki's main square. She Googled the name of the restaurant, Taverna Gardenia, and I scribbled a note on my train ticket.

A change in trains and a short taxi ride – shared with the Americans from our carriage – brought me, exhausted, to Doupiani House in the village of Kastraki. This was a lovely hotel, but it had no restaurant except for the breakfast room, and I was too downhearted to hang out in its bar or venture into the night to find the feast I'd been anticipating. The cheese, nuts and bottle of wine I'd picked up in the Athens supermarket that morning would have to do.

The first drinking glass I picked up slipped from my hand and shattered. The wine turned out to be too sweet for my taste, but I sipped at it anyway as I gathered up the shards. An online check of my bank account didn't show any irregular transactions, but it was too soon to be sure. After an unsatisfying supper of supermarket snacks, I turned in for an early night, putting an end to a day filled with disappointments and frustrations. My morale was low, but I was determined tomorrow would be better.

# CHAPTER ELEVEN
# METEORA'S WORLD
# HERITAGE

A FEW WEEKS BEFORE I left Australia, two friends upset the itinerary I'd worked so hard to put together. Daniel and Rebecca have never met, but he had been to Greece recently, she as a child. Within hours of each other, they urged me to visit Meteora. They were both so smitten with their memories that I changed my schedule. It took two long, travel-filled days to squeeze in thirty-six hours in this surreal natural landscape marked by extraordinary human settlement.

Meteora sits on about seven hundred acres of the Thessalian plain in central Greece, in the foothills of the Pindus range of mountains. What makes it unique are the massive rock formations peppered across this plain – together with how they've been inhabited. Some are towering columns of stone, reaching hundreds of metres into the air. Others appear to be free-standing pillars when viewed from the front, but merge into sloping grassy plateaus behind them. Still others are boulder-like hills marked with eerie furrows and folds. This area was once underwater, maybe as long as sixty million years ago, and, over the aeons, currents and flows carved the stone into strange shapes. After tectonic forces pushed the seabed upwards, the climate took over the job, weathering the exposed rock into the sculpted forms that define this landscape.

People have deemed this area holy for more than a thousand years. Christian hermits first scaled these heights to make their dwellings in cavities in the stone pillars at the turn of the last millennium – possibly even as far back as the triple-digit years, before the year 1000 in the Common Era. As the world grew increasingly dangerous, more and more monks sought the safety of Meteora's inaccessible peaks. They started building monasteries here in the fourteenth century, around the time the Ottomans began encroaching on the Byzantine Empire.

These religious communities thrived and multiplied over the fifteenth and sixteenth centuries, resulting in two dozen monasteries built on and in the rocks. Places of safety, they were reached by rope ladders or in large nets the monks used to haul both people and goods from the ground. This was not for the fainthearted, given the oft-quoted response attributed to a long-ago monk when asked how frequently they replaced the nets: 'When the Lord lets them break.'

Although there were once twenty-four religious communities living in Meteora's monasteries, their numbers have decreased since the seventeenth century. Today, only half a dozen of the monasteries house religious orders. All six are open to the public, but I had no idea how long it would take to travel from one to another, or how much time I would need at each. I set a realistic goal: a meaningful visit to at least two of the monasteries.

There was one I knew I wouldn't be visiting: Moni Agias Triados wasn't open on Thursdays. This was the monastic community where an unexpected turn of twentieth-century events altered Meteora's future.

The twelfth James Bond movie, *For Your Eyes Only* starring Roger Moore, hit the screens in 1981. Typical of the 007 franchise, it was a box-office success, despite being so cheesy as to be cringeworthy. (An ingénue character named Bibi Dahl? Really?) Its climactic scene is set in Moni Agias Triados, and the film's burst into popular culture brought a tourism boom to the region.

Many of the monks were against shooting the movie in their hallowed places. When a court case failed to stop production, some tried to sabotage the film by hanging laundry from their windows whenever the cameras were ready to roll.

For a thousand years, Meteora had offered an escape from a vulgar world, but the aftermath of the blockbuster saw an influx of tourism that impacted the fabric of monastic life, even as it enriched the churches' coffers. Many monks left the area to seek solitude elsewhere, some on the 335-square-kilometre peninsula of Mount Athos. The Greek Orthodox Church protects *that* enclave with such ferocity that its thousand-year-old prohibition on women applies not only to human visitors of all ages but also to mares, hens, sows and nanny-goats – but not to female insects, wild birds or, surprisingly, cats. I guess cats just get to do whatever they want, wherever they might be.

By 2015, only fifteen monks lived in four of Meteora's monasteries. The other two active communities became nuns' convents in 1961 and 1988.

~ ~ ~

On awakening, I threw open the curtains and patio doors, revealing a mysterious vista of bulbous rock towers scattered across the fanciful topography. In the dark of my arrival, I'd been too disheartened to pay attention to my erratic surroundings. Now, they filled me with joy. I flicked on my phone to post a photograph:

> 22 September 2016
> On my way out to hike this awe-inspiring landscape. Got my *kefi* back :-)

*Kefi* is a Greek word and concept that, I've read, is difficult to translate into English. It means something like 'high spirits', and I really had got over the horrible slump that had overtaken me the day before. The sweltering heat had broken for the first time since I'd arrived in Greece, and the misty morning called to me.

The knitting journalist I'd met at Limnisa had spent a few nights in Meteora, coincidentally at this very hotel, before coming to the writers' retreat. She'd recommended a guided walking tour, which seemed just the thing for this blissfully cool day. Christina at the reception desk, who had answered my many emailed questions over the past few weeks with generous patience, brushed aside my apologies for the broken wineglass and offered to phone the tour guide to book my place.

Before venturing out, I wanted breakfast. Doupiani House, recommended for its magnificent views and reasonable prices, was also renowned for its splendid morning buffets. The knitting journalist had confirmed that these breakfasts were indeed marvellous. Together, we'd convinced two of our fellow guests that it would be the perfect place to break their journey to the Pelion Peninsula.

Denise and Bill were American pastors. They were also community activists, and their company was as interesting as it was agreeable. At Limnisa, when we'd discussed Jeffrey Eugenides' superb novel *Middlesex*, Bill had talked about the book's depiction of the 1967 riot in Detroit, where he lived, and his own memories of this event.

They had left Limnisa halfway through my stay. If their journey had gone according to plan, Denise and Bill would now be here in Meteora, preparing to travel onward. We had a loose arrangement to meet up for breakfast if our visits coincided and, sure enough, I ran into them at the juice stand. The outside tables were wet from the night's rainfall, but we preferred to sit in the quiet garden rather than in the busy breakfast room surrounded by chatter, and the hotel staff were quick to wipe down the furniture as soon as they noticed us heading outdoors. It was a merry reunion, and an hour flew by as we compared travel notes over eggs, regional sausages and cheeses, fresh-baked breads, local honey and jams, and the rich aroma of coffee.

As I made my way back to my bedroom to grab my daypack for the hike, Christina intercepted me with the disappointing news that the guide had cancelled today's walking tour. The reason? The weather. Someone had judged this lovely day, promising a mix of sunshine and occasional sprinkles of light rainfall, to be unsuitable for walking.

Christina proposed a solution. She pulled out a small-scale tourist map of the area. It wasn't designed to guide a hiker around the multiple walking trails through the rock formations, but she picked up a pen and outlined a basic route to Moni Megalou Meteorou, which, at 613 metres above sea level, is the highest of the monasteries. She listed the landmarks by which I should steer my course and warned me to take a detour around Doupiani Rock itself, as it would be dangerously slippery in the rain.

To be honest, her instructions passed in a blur. I wasn't clear on the paths I'd need to follow, but I was game to give it a go. Clutching the map, I set out, skirting Doupiani Rock and heading up the tarred road.

The countryside was deserted in the soft morning light, the rhythm of my footsteps marking my progress past a closed taverna, a donkey tied to a tree, a pack of inquisitive dogs. There was also a sign confirming that UNESCO had added the Archaeological Site of Meteora to the World Heritage List in 1988.

~ ~ ~

UNESCO is the United Nations agency that focuses on education, science and culture. It manages the World Heritage List, an inventory of more than a thousand places on our planet deemed so valuable that they deserve to belong not just to one country or one generation, but to the heritage of the entire world.

Famous World Heritage Sites include the Grand Canyon in the United States, the Great Wall of China, Stonehenge in the United Kingdom, and the ancient cities of Damascus and

Aleppo in Syria, which are now under grave threat. Also on the list is Mosi-oa-Tunya – which translates as 'The Smoke that Thunders' and is better known as Victoria Falls – on the border between Zimbabwe and Zambia. Australia has twenty listings, including two that flirt with each other, at a chaste arm's length, for hundreds of parallel kilometres: the Wet Tropics of Queensland on land, and the Great Barrier Reef in the ocean. India's Taj Mahal, which I'd visited with Adam earlier that year, and Machu Picchu in Peru, where I'd walked with my sisters fifteen years before, are on the list too.

Years ago, I worked for a heritage consultancy based in Cape Town. It was an exciting time. South Africa was re-emerging onto the world stage after its era of isolation, when international sanctions had been a powerful weapon against apartheid. In 1999, our fledgling democracy – welcomed back into the global community after decades of economic, cultural and sporting boycotts – celebrated its first three inscriptions on the World Heritage List.

One of these was a collection of palaeontological excavation sites nicknamed the Cradle of Humankind and, as a young researcher in a dream job, I played a minuscule role in the master-planning phase for its visitor centre. Part of my work included reporting on other World Heritage Sites around the world so we could learn from their experiences. This was all desktop research, using card catalogues in libraries and navigating my way around a rudimentary internet.

Ever since, whenever I've been lucky enough to travel, I have checked the World Heritage List to see if I'd be able to visit any of these sites. For this trip, I turned that pattern on its head. For months, grappling with an undefined but persistent discontent, I'd craved adventure, a chance to travel solo to an exotic destination. I knew I needed to challenge myself, and especially my fear of bus travel, but I hadn't a clue where to go. I was trapped in the stagnant quicksand of my own inertia.

One day, on a lunch break at my desk, I pulled up the UNESCO website on my phone and scanned the World Heritage List. The instant my eyes rested on the entries for Greece, I knew *this* was where I needed to go. A month later, I was there.

~ ~ ~

To be included on the World Heritage List, a site must meet at least one of ten criteria: six cultural measures and four natural ones.

At the time of my visit, there were 1,052 World Heritage-listed properties scattered across 165 countries. More than eight hundred of these were Cultural Sites. A much lower number, around two hundred, were Natural Sites. A tiny portion, just three percent, were labelled as Mixed. These thirty-five properties, spread over twenty-seven countries worldwide, were extraordinary among a list of already-extraordinary sites. They satisfied criteria for outstanding universal value, deserving of protection for the benefit of all humanity for all time, in both the cultural and natural categories.

Meteora, I discovered from the roadside sign, ticked five of the criteria boxes across both categories, making it an exceptional treasure. And here was I, that little girl who grew up in a narrow world in the sheltered suburbs of Cape Town, stepping out to encounter it.

The word 'extraordinary' has cropped up a few times in this chapter, but there's a reason for this. It's a word I often ponder, and it was on my mind throughout my exploration of Greece.

A few years before, when my workplace was going through yet another bruising restructure, I attended a talk on resilience. These corporate courses are often fluffy nonsense wrapped in a clever package, but this one was different. The facilitator, Dominic Siow, had us laughing for the full three hours. This was therapeutic in itself, but he also gave us a lot to consider. What struck me – and then stayed with me – was a question he had us ask ourselves. *One day, when I am old and I look back over the years, what will I see that has made my life extraordinary?*

The answer would be as unique as each person seeking it. It might not appear rare or unusual from an outsider's perspective. But it could change the direction of that person's life, and the achievement of its potential would mean more to them than anything else they had accomplished. For Dominic and his wife, it had been choosing parenthood over the trajectories of their successful Silicon Valley careers. What could it be for me?

It was a question that had bedevilled me in recent months, while I struggled with the middlescent banality of my life. In that moment, as I gazed around at the pillars of Meteora, I wondered: *Is this my answer? Could it be travel – fearless travel or, rather, travel in spite of my fears – that makes my life extraordinary?*

I stood at a crossroads, my feet anchored to the steep vehicle-access road climbing to the monasteries. The closest, Moni Agiou Nikolaou, sat in majesty on its rocky summit up ahead, but – just as shown in ballpoint pen on my map – a path led off to the left, flanked on both sides by misty woodlands and soaring rocky pinnacles. It was something less than a road but more than a track.

I looked to the smooth road ahead, so sure of its route, and then again at the uncertain trail. That was where my feet wanted to take me, and I wasn't going to argue. I took a step. And then another.

# CHAPTER TWELVE
## MONOPATIA AND MOUSSAKA
## IN METEORA

MONI AGIOU NIKOLAOU TOWERED over the trail, looking as if it were suspended in the gleaming grey heavens. There were unexpected symmetries at its summit: a manicured tree and what looked curiously like a Victorian bandstand, or at least some kind of gazebo. On each side of my path were forests and valleys and, everywhere, the monolithic outcrops, wreathed in tendrils of mist.

It was so good to be out, alone, moving, breathing the fresh countryside air. Clumsy as I am, I still trust my feet far more than I could ever trust the wheels of a bus or any other vehicle. The walk was grounding me with every step.

There was a crossroads, then another, both corresponding reassuringly with tracks shown on the map. I passed a tiny shrine and a few more turnoffs, and the course became less clear. I kept to the main trail, wondering if I'd missed my turn but not yet concerned. After a field of beehives came a definite fork in the road, at about the spot where my pen-sketched route left the edge of the page. The ink line reappeared within millimetres, looping to the right, but, for the moment, I'd dropped off the edge of the charted world. I hesitated.

Some distance ahead stood a larger shrine topped by a cross. Christina had mentioned a 'monument' where I should turn and had cautioned that this was where some people lose their way. *Could this be it?*

To my left, a half-toppled sign in Greek script showed a stylised image of a man aiming a rifle, circled in red with a bold diagonal strike-through. *No hunting allowed, maybe?* Unsure whether this was a good omen or a disquieting one – a warning of random shots fired – I examined the turnoff. A simple metal bar partway across the trail blocked access to vehicles, but there was no indication that pedestrians shouldn't pass. I had a hunch this was the right way, and I took the turn.

Within minutes, I felt the almost physical sensation of my heart lifting, along with my gaze, at the wondrous sight ahead. Hugging the cliff face high above, an isolated monastery peered down at me from under its looming brow of overhanging rock. Consulting the map, I identified it – incorrectly, as it turned out – as Agios Dimitrios.

In fact, it was the monastery of Ypapanti, founded in the fourteenth century. The ruins of Agios Dimitrios sit far above Ypapanti, and I didn't see them during my wanderings, although I'd later find them when zooming in on scenic photographs.

Both religious communities were important actors in the nineteenth-century struggle against the occupying Ottoman Empire. Agios Dimitrios served as a fortress during the local uprising, while Ypapanti suffered significant punitive damage during the 1809 capture of Papa Thymios Vlachavas. This rebel warrior-monk was seized by the forces of an Albanian warlord turned Ottoman governor, Ali Pasha of Ioannina, whom the poet Lord Byron called the 'Muslim Bonaparte' and who was also known as *Aslan*.

*Aslan*, by the way, is Turkish for 'the Lion' – a little linguistic treat for those of us who, as children, immersed ourselves in *The Chronicles of Narnia*.

Unlike the active monasteries I was seeking, Ypapanti didn't sit atop one of the massive stone pillars. Instead, the building's facade clung to the side of a cliff, its chambers extending deep into caves in the rock. Although unoccupied, the monastery has been restored, and its neat stone exterior was beautiful.

There was a metal elevator high above me, a recent replacement for the precarious ropes of the past, with sturdy cables leading to a stone shed at the base of the rock. Further investigation revealed steep steps climbing to a locked front door. Modern renovators had constructed this fine staircase to make the abandoned monastery more accessible on the one day of the year it was open to the public: the feast of the presentation of the forty-day-old infant Jesus in the temple. The Greek Orthodox Church celebrates this holy day, known as Ypapanti, in February.

From the top of the stairs, I looked over the trees at a boulder-like hill with an enormous cross at its crest and, nearby, a larger-than-life-sized statue. This, and not the shrine I'd seen before, was obviously the monument Christina had mentioned. The serene solitude of Ypapanti had been a bonus, but it was time to get going. To stay on the correct course, I would have to choose my way with care.

I had moved beyond the area of the map that was of any practical use to hikers. The paths were narrower, there were more of them, and all I could tell from my annotated map was that I would need to follow one of the trails curving around to the right. While the first part of this gentle hike had been a country lane, these were the real *monopatia,* or monk paths, that wound through fields and forests, around and even up the great stone formations.

I took three wrong turns and had to backtrack each time.

One path led to a shrine enclosing an icon of Saint George on his white steed, rearing above a dragon breathing red tongues of flame. The saint was frozen in an instant of crisis:

his red cloak streamed behind him, his white-tipped spear about to pierce the reptile's jaw, but he hadn't noticed the scaly tail coiled around his mount's hind leg. *Is the dragon planning, perhaps, to bring down the horse and unseat the rider?*

The second turn took me to the feet of a grim-faced Greek Orthodox monk. This was the statue I'd seen from Ypapanti, and how I'd arrived at its foot was a mystery, as I'd set out in quite the opposite direction. It depicted Papa Thymios Vlachavas, the heroic monk from the early-nineteenth-century resistance who was captured at the monastery across the valley and executed, his body hacked into gruesome pieces.

My third attempt was the lucky one, but, even then, a narrow path lured me off the trail. This detour brought me to a plateau littered with cowpats, though there wasn't a cow in sight. Returning to the track, I came a cropper, slipping off a wet rock and bruising my knee. I gave silent thanks to Christina for warning me away from Doupiani Rock, which would have been treacherous to cross in the fine rain.

I was still limping when I crossed paths with a party of four walkers who reassured me that I was going the right way. Happily 'following my nose', just as my grandmother taught me, I'd been walking for two hours, and, apart from a group of three hikers I had seen in the distance earlier, these were the first humans I'd encountered. It felt as if I were miles from anywhere, but, minutes later, my breath caught at the glimpse of a monastery through the greenery. Then I stepped out of the wilderness, finding myself above a road filled with coachload upon coachload of tourists. The stink of fuel tainted the air, and jarring voices shouted above the thrum of idling engines.

It was a bit of a scramble down from the trail, and I slid the last couple of metres on my backside to join the hordes. As much as I might dislike the conveyer-belt feel of mass tourism, in the end I was a tourist just like everybody else. *Sometimes you have to take the tourist track to engage with our world's greatest wonders,* I reminded myself. *This is one of those times.*

~ ~ ~

The monasteries stand like steeple crosses atop spires of stone. Until early in the last century, monks hauled their guests up in rope nets. Thanks to the innovations of the 1920s, I could now haul myself up flight after flight (after flight, after flight) of stairs to visit two of the largest monasteries, Moni Megalou Meteorou and Moni Varlaam.

At the first, an emphatic sign greeted visitors in misspelled capital letters: 'SHORTS ARE NOT ALLOWED. LADIES IN SLEVELESS DRESSES, SLACKS OR PANTALOONS WILL NOT BE ADMITTED.' The archaic word gave me a silent giggle, but I'd come prepared. I'd already pulled a maxi skirt from my backpack to cover my leggings, and, as always when travelling, I carried a light shawl in case I needed additional cover for my head or shoulders. But, not for the first time and not for the last, the arrogance of some tourists astounded me.

Granted, not everyone has a guidebook to give them a heads-up on the expected etiquette. Not everyone, even, has the common sense or cultural awareness to foresee that a religious site might call for a modest dress code. I could understand why someone might be tempted to bend the rules if they had travelled around the world for a once-in-a-lifetime experience and hadn't known in advance that, for example, ladies' pantaloons weren't welcome. I'm not saying it's okay, but I get it.

What I don't get is why, when the helpful monk at the door was handing out sarongs to both men and women who didn't meet the dress requirements, so many people discarded them as soon as they turned the corner. Forlorn strips of cloth littered the ground.

Another notice read: 'You are entering a living monastery. These grounds are sacred and you are asked to show reverence during your visit.' Many lowered their voices as they moved about this place of worship, tempering their natural curiosity with respect. But with the cast-off sarongs and the raucous group clanging the bell in the courtyard, I felt a certain shame on behalf of travellers everywhere.

Annoying sightseers aside, these two monasteries, perched on the rocks not far from each other, were a delight. There were reconstructions of the old kitchens and storage cellars. Small museums showcased church treasures and artefacts from Greece's historic rebellions and battles. Photographic exhibitions compared the day-to-day lives of monks hundreds of years in the past to those of today. In an arched alcove, putting the finishing touches to a mural, a blue-jeaned artist wielded his brush.

In one stone-walled room stood an enormous wooden barrel. I was crushed to learn it wasn't a wine cask; it had been skilfully crafted to store up to twelve tonnes of rainwater. A sign reading 'TO THE NET' pointed to the site of a bygone lifting mechanism, where builders were using an only slightly more modern electric motor to winch up materials for renovations. And the churches! Glorious murals, depicting thousands of images of saints and martyrs in vibrant colours, covered every inch of the interior walls.

A fleeting look at the ossuary – and the voyeuristic tourists clustered around it – got me thinking about the complex ethics around displaying human remains, even as I acknowledged their morbid attraction. I didn't yet understand how, here in Greece, this public preservation of the dead could be an act of veneration.

Above all, from every window and courtyard, the views of the eerie terrain plunging down to the valley floor were breathtaking. I didn't rush, preferring to soak in the atmosphere. Nevertheless, even though I'd thought these might be the only monasteries I would have the capacity to visit, my solitary walk had energised me and there was plenty of time to keep exploring.

Leaving the crowds behind, I followed the road downhill to a community with a very different energy from the testosterone-drenched buildings I'd just visited. Originally a monastery founded in the mid-sixteenth century, it has been known as the holy nunnery of Agias Varvaras-Rousanou since 1988. I wondered what the monks of Mount Athos thought about that.

A narrow pedestrian bridge spanned the chasm that gaped before the entrance to the convent, which felt precariously balanced on its natural stone pillar. Its church was small, but the frescoes were superb, and the antechamber was peaceful and welcoming. A smiling nun sold me a fridge magnet – a rare keepsake, as I've never been a great purchaser of souvenirs. This one was for Megan, my closest friend since we met at our Catholic school three decades earlier. Had she seen me hesitating at the little bridge, she would have told me to put on my 'big girl panties' and stride across with my head held high.

We are polar opposites, in many ways, but she's my sister in spirit. She lives halfway across the world from me, and it took a couple of years before this token found its home in her kitchen.

~ ~ ~

Down the steps I went and further down the wide, winding road. The day was wearing on, and I was tired to the bone – both physically, from the hiking and climbing, and mentally, from absorbing so much history. Even my eyes were tired from examining the minuscule details of illuminated walls.

There would be time for one more stop on the way back to the hotel: the tiny monastery dedicated to Saint Nicholas that had watched over that morning's trail. When I arrived at the base of its rock tower, though, a sign informed me that – unlike the other monasteries I'd visited that day, all of which closed at five o'clock – this one would shut its doors at four. I told myself it was too late, then battled up the steep stairs anyway, my heartbeat thudding painfully. An internal debate raged with every upward step. *Is it worth racing the clock?* When I got to the top, legs on fire and chest heaving, the cranky young monk who took my three euros told me they'd be closing in ten minutes.

Moni Agiou Nikolaou is the smallest of the active monasteries, so I was able to hurry through its public spaces, taking in as much as I could, and stand atop the same summit I had glanced up at that morning. It only took a second to work out that the 'gazebo' I'd seen earlier was a freestanding brick belfry.

Nine minutes after I'd handed over the coins, when I told the monk that the frescoes here were the finest I'd seen that day, his grumpy face cracked into the sweetest smile.

Footsore but hungry after eight strenuous hours on my feet – given the austere squat toilet I'd visited around midday, I didn't even get to sit down to pee – I bypassed the turnoff to my hotel and wandered into the village of Kastraki in search of Taverna Gardenia. My Greek fellow passenger on the train had urged me to try their *païdakia*, but the waiter explained it was not a good time of year for lamb cutlets.

'Come back at Easter or in November,' he said. He recommended the moussaka instead.

Its aroma arrived first, a mouth-watering promise of garlic and a tang of tomato. The waiter wasn't far behind, sliding the steaming dish onto the table with a flourish. After the first forkful of minced beef layered with eggplant and a creamy béchamel sauce, I closed my eyes, all the better to savour the subtle harmony of tastes and textures. A local white wine came with the food, and I polished off two glasses before it rushed to my head. With regret, I left the rest in the half-litre carafe and gathered my belongings, taking care to unhook the Peruvian water bottle sling from the back of my chair. I'd misplaced and later recovered this precious memento all over the world – in a Prague restaurant with Shauna, on a Pacific cruise ship with Tassin – and I didn't want to lose it in Greece.

On just the right side of tipsy, I limped back to Doupiani House to take a much-needed shower and tuck my weary feet into bed. When I emptied my pockets, Megan's little magnet rattled onto the bedside table like a teaspoon in a cup, stirring up a brew from the past.

Perhaps the nostalgia was a by-product of the potent wine with my meal, but it set my thoughts skipping between the women in my life. As I clicked off the light and waited for sleep to wrap its arms around my aching limbs, my mind settled on the memory that had been simmering since I'd read Jenny's Facebook comment ten days before: our family rite of passage gone wrong in Peru.

Instead of three sisters and a niece sharing a four-day trek through the mountains to the fabulous ruins of Machu Picchu, we'd separated in alarming circumstances when Jenny became unwell on the Inca Trail. Tassin and Lee-Ann, mother and daughter, had completed the hike. Jenny and I turned back to Cuzco, the town the Inca considered to be the navel of the Earth. It was an anxious, hundred-kilometre journey on foot, by bus, and in a beat-up old taxi. Our jovial driver swivelled the radio's volume dial to the right, until the cheerful music competed with his own laughing banter. Meanwhile, Jenny and I gripped our seats as the car hurtled through the deepening dusk, headlights off, and my agitated warnings about cows in our path built to a shrieked, '¡Hay vacas! ¡Hay vacas!'

Although I didn't get to fulfil my dream of hiking through the Andes to celebrate my birthday, my thirtieth year marked a new phase in my relationship with my sisters, who'd moved out of home when I was a child. Peru was where we connected as adults, as individuals and as friends, rather than as nominal siblings.

That's when my reverie ruptured, and I sat up with a start. The whole point of that expedition had been the birthdays – it was 2001, the year of Lee-Ann's twenty-first, my thirtieth and Tassin's fortieth. We'd decreed that Jenny's birthday was special too; she was about to turn the neat double-digit age of forty-four.

*I* was forty-four during this Greek trip, just three months short of my forty-fifth. I knocked my mother's diary to the floor while fumbling for the light switch, but I soon got it open to the inside cover with its handwritten dates. Mum was forty-five when she was here, in Greece.

As I studied the handwriting, so familiar from the household shopping lists and school permission slips of my childhood, something shifted inside me and my mother emerged from the page. Perhaps for the first time, I recognised her as a woman of flesh and blood, aspirations and frustrations. Like Jenny – like me – she had set out on a journey to a foreign land in her middlescence, to discover the unknown and maybe a little piece of herself.

# CHAPTER THIRTEEN
# METEORA TO THE CAULDRON
# OF SANTORINI

**T**HE FOUR-HOUR BUS RIDE to Thessaloniki was uneventful, marked only by a seemingly pointless halt at a service station, leading to a voluble argument between a few of the passengers. It turned out we'd made this unscheduled stop because a young man had been in urgent need of a toilet. One passenger, frustrated at the lengthy wait, let forth a tirade of protest at the delay. The others argued it could happen to anyone; one day she, too, might be grateful for an understanding driver if she were ever caught short. The driver himself maintained a steadfast silence, declining to enter the debate, and the quarrel ended with the sheepish return of the shamefaced passenger.

Thessaloniki, Greece's second largest city, was the northernmost point of my itinerary. I had first encountered it in the pages of Victoria Hislop's novel *The Thread* and then, in much greater detail, in Mark Mazower's non-fiction masterpiece, *Salonica: City of Ghosts*. These were the books that introduced me to the 'population exchange' of the early twentieth century. This innocuous term hides the trauma of two million people, in two countries, being torn from their homes.

In the League of Nations' 1923 Treaty of Lausanne, the stroke of a well-meaning pen classed entire communities in Turkey and Greece as non-citizens and banished them from the only lands they had ever known. Both governments agreed to categorise Muslims as Turks and Christians as Greeks, regardless of the language they spoke or where the bones of their ancestors rested. Coerced evacuations took place, in often-brutal conditions, as the two populations were exchanged. Many families left on foot, at short notice, carrying infants, the elderly, and not much else.

The early pages of *The Thread* enchanted me with its depiction of the city's multiculturalism, before the population exchange and the later Nazi Holocaust devastated its Muslim and Jewish communities. How I would have loved a leisurely ramble around Thessaloniki, looking for traces of its cultural heritage as well as the new diversity of the twenty-first century. Sadly, I was merely passing through. Even though I hoped the airport shuttle might at least drive past the White Tower, I didn't get a glimpse of the city's most iconic structure. There really was a bus strike in Thessaloniki, and the only way to get to my plane was an expensive one: by taxi.

Fortunately, a strident Englishwoman waiting in the long queue for a taxi identified me as a likely candidate for a trip to the airport. She had previously lived in Greece for several decades and was here on one of her frequent visits to her adult son. She was on her way to catch a flight home, but her plans had also been disrupted by the bus strike. She bustled me over to her spot in the queue and informed me that we'd share a ride. Even if I had wanted to refuse, I wouldn't have dared. She spoke fluent Greek to the taxi driver and got us to our destination very efficiently indeed. We split the fare, with her pressing coins back into my hands as she muttered about over-tipping.

Repeated checks of my bank's online statements had shown no suspicious five-hundred-euro deductions from my account and, by now, my need for cash was critical. I'd found it was often the preferred – and sometimes the only – method of payment. But Thessaloniki airport was a small one, and a thorough search didn't reveal any staffed banks. There was nothing for it; I'd have to take my chances with another ATM.

Once again, the machine spat the card out in disgust, but this time a message flashed up on the screen: 'Insufficient Funds'.

This made no sense. I'd organised my multicurrency travelcard for this very purpose, and it held precisely five hundred euros – my remaining budget for this trip – as well as a comfortable balance in Australian dollars for emergencies.

Then it struck me: the bank fee was pushing me over my euro limit! I tried again, this time asking for just 480 euros. The money emerged from its slot, and my anxieties over the phantom withdrawal in Athens evaporated.

I used the last few euros on my card to buy a mediocre *pastitsio* lunch of pasta and meat sauce, then joined what may have been the sweatiest, most claustrophobic and slowest-moving queue of my life. After inching my way through the airport security checkpoint, I got to the boarding gate and whipped out my phone:

> 23 September 2016
>
> Waiting to board. Very hot. Very crowded. Plane very small. But today an old lady blessed me for helping her get a large parcel out of the bus. At least, I think it was a blessing: it involved the sign of the cross. Guess it can't hurt.

~ ~ ~

When I cobbled together my itinerary, I had been more excited about Santorini than any of the other destinations. This wasn't because I knew much about it; it was because of its *name*. Santorini… it slides from your mouth with a magical hiss and roll. The sound evokes sandalwood and spice and exotic elixir and passion.

When I put out a call for suggestions of places to visit in Greece, I received a prompt response from someone I hadn't seen since we were at school. Ruby was the younger sister of Tasso, who was my brother's classmate and the subject of my first sustained pre-adolescent crush. Well, the second, if you count my earlier obsession with Boy George. My unrequited infatuation with Tasso lingered well into my teenage years and became a high school friendship.

By now, that was ancient history. Ruby was all grown up and living in Greece. We wouldn't be able to meet up during my travels. She was away on her own holiday, and our paths would cross just days from each other. But she put me in touch with her sister-in-law, Fotini, who lived on Santorini in a house with two adjoining Airbnb apartments.

Despite one wrong turn that took me towing my damaged suitcase around the block, it was easy to find Folia Apartments. Because Fotini was out at her day job as a wedding planner – weddings are a major industry on Santorini – her mother unlocked the door and shepherded me into Folia's cool rooms. The ground-floor flat was right in the middle of Fira, Santorini's main town, but it was a restful sanctuary from the buzz of tourism. And what a luxury it was, after weeks in single rooms, to have an entire apartment in which to spread out, even a fully equipped kitchen.

Yeah, as if I was going to be doing any cooking. Still, you do need somewhere to store the pistachios and pour the wine.

Dozens of online testimonials bear witness to Fotini's friendly service and hospitable touch. She respects her guests' privacy but makes herself available for anything they might need. Having someone willing to make a few phone calls in Greek, to help with enquiries and reservations, can make all the difference. While I received the same sterling service as her other paying guests, I had the additional benefit of being treated as a friend of the family, with her mother insisting on keeping a plate of dinner for me and (bless her) washing a load of my grubby laundry.

~ ~ ~

On my first morning in Santorini, I switched off my alarm long before it sounded. I wasn't sure what this day would bring, but I did know it would start with a four-hour walk along the caldera to Oia.

The word 'caldera' brings to mind an image of a seething cauldron, and that's not far off in either shape or volatility; a caldera is the hollow formed when a volcano caves in. Just as the Acropolis in Athens has special status, distinguished from hundreds of other acropolises with its uppercase A, the ocean-filled caldera of Santorini deserves distinction. In Greece, this is *the* caldera.

As for the village of Oia, which I soon learned to pronounce 'ee-ya', it is the perfect picture of a Greek island: a cascade of white houses trimmed in blue, tumbling from a clifftop to the deep waters below. Since masses of tourists flock to Oia for its sunsets, my aim was to enjoy a brief mosey around the town and get out of there straight after lunch.

The walk to Oia was ground-breaking.

To describe Santorini, I have to begin with the remarkable landscape. Actually, I'll go back a step further, to the island's name. Santorini, with its exquisite, sibilant sounds that slip from the tongue and enticed me across the world, isn't really called Santorini at all. Its true modern designation is Thira, and this is how you'll find it listed on airplane tickets and official documents. 'Santorini' comes from '*Santa Irini*' and dates from the era of the crusades. Thirteenth-century Venetian occupiers dubbed the island after the chapel to Agia Irini, or Saint Irene, which stood near the bay where they moored their boats.

Thira has had several names over the ages, but the most descriptive was its ancient moniker, Strogili (sometimes written as Strongili), meaning 'round'. This is what it was called four thousand years ago, before the cataclysm that changed its shape.

In around 1600 BCE, give or take a hundred years, a volcanic event of catastrophic proportions tore the circular island to pieces. Its middle plummeted into the sea, creating the ocean-filled crater now called the caldera. Some scientists believe this may have been the most powerful eruption to have taken place on our planet in the last five millennia.

Disastrous as it was, the Minoan eruption was not, in geological terms, an isolated incident.

It was not the first time volcanic activity had crumbled the island, leaving small islets in a ring around the watery heart of the volcano, and then gradually refilled the crater with volcanic material. The island's disintegration may have been a direct result of the explosions. Or it might have been the weight of accumulated rock resting atop empty magma chambers – hollowed out by the eruptions – that caused it to collapse into the sea. Whatever the exact mechanism, geological evidence indicates this has been a cyclical process repeated over hundreds of thousands of years.

What makes this particular event so significant to us, as human beings subject to the capricious forces of nature, is that there was an advanced human civilisation on Strogili at that time. The centre of this civilisation was a town named Akrotiri.

Some have argued that Santorini's volatile history makes Akrotiri the most plausible site for the legendary land of Atlantis. The white, red and black stone in Plato's fourth-century BCE account – corresponding to the striking colours of three famous beaches near Akrotiri – is intriguing circumstantial evidence. Santorini is only one of dozens of hypothesised locations for the mythical island that sank into the sea, though, so I wouldn't get too excited about it.

Back to the terrain. The Minoan eruption left three islands: Thira stretching around the eastern edge of the bowl, Thirasia cupping part of its north-western quadrant, and the tiny fragment of Aspronisi, lonely in the south-west. These three clearly show the rim of the volcano, poking up through hundreds of fathoms of water. Over the next two millennia, Palia Kameni and Nea Kameni formed in the centre. The five islands make up the archipelago of Santorini we know today.

This simplistic geological overview sets the scene for my walk from Fira to Oia.

Fira rests on the lip of the caldera, two-thirds of the way up the crescent-shaped island of Thira. Oia sits at the northern tip of the crescent, where it curls to the west. The walk along the windswept edge provided an ever-changing view as I arced around the crater, with an arid plateau spreading far below to my right, and striated cliffs plunging into the sea to my left. Currents played with glinting sunlight and deep blue shadows.

My visual perspective of the island evolved as I moved along the curve. As I skirted the luxury hotels and cocktail bars of the caldera, their infinity pools shimmering in the morning sun, another perspective was also evolving.

There was hardly anyone about, and it was too early for the cliff-edge pools to be disturbed by bronzed bodies, probably still sleeping off the previous night's excesses. I cast my eye over lodgings I could never afford, my thoughts progressing through a series of steps:

*So, this is how the other half travels.*

*No, wait, that can't be correct. Not the other half. Those numbers don't even begin to add up. It's more like the Occupy movement, with their Guy Fawkes masks and their hashtag #WeAreThe99Percent.*

*So, this is how the One Percent travels.*

*Hmm, let's do the calculations. In Australia, I would rank as lower-middle class, or some such term — it's not a very classist society. I'm far from wealthy, though, and I earn a salary well below the national average. Even below the average for women, which is about fifteen percent lower than that for men.*

*But in terms of the freedom and financial means to travel the globe, compared to the world population, I might be within the One Percent.*

This thought shocked me right out of my self-indulgent midlife crisis. How arrogant I'd been, disgruntled with my life when I was one of the favoured few! In a split second, my recent malaise — that indefinable dissatisfaction that had plagued my middlescence — dissolved into nothing. The nagging question, 'Is this enough?' slunk away with its tail between its legs.

# CHAPTER FOURTEEN
## SANTORINI SUNSET

A s I CRESTED THE final hill, passing the path's last glowing white chapel, I was looking forward to a cold drink and – you know me by now – something scrumptious for lunch. Battling Santorini's famous wind on the more exposed parts of the track had burned through the last of my energy. It wasn't long, though, until the architectural effect of Oia's narrow main thoroughfare revived my spirits.

There was a shop set below the caldera path, the words 'Fashion & art' picked out in blue against its dazzling walls. Four outdoor mannequins modelled flowing garments in black and white, red, blue and yellow, fluttering to dramatic effect against the backdrop of the rippling waters far below.

A few minutes later, I came across Atlantis Books, so strikingly decorated both inside and out that it was a magnet for photographers. Depictions of gloriously shambolic bookshelves covered its exterior walls, which bore a bold sign proclaiming, 'Rent A Cat'. At the top of a stone stairway, leading down to the bookshop's entrance in a tiny courtyard, sat a bowl of coins labelled: 'Photographers! Please feel very welcome to use your camera here. Donations here will help us keep our lights on and doors open for all photographers and booklovers.'

The store was a warren of shelves filled with an eclectic array of books ranging from valuable first editions of international classics to a section classified as Greek Interest. Stacks of books were labelled with handwritten staff recommendations: 'The best Greek cookbook of all time!' and 'So good. And don't worry, it's not all depressing or anything.'

The air was redolent with the heavy scent of books, the walls inscribed with quotes and a timeline of the shop owners' lives. The list of dates recorded the establishment of the store, the adoption of their cats, the first Caldera Arts & Literature Festival and, in joyous letters, a wedding. There was a 'GREAT FLOOD (Don't ask)' and a summer 'so scorching hot that we carve a HOLE in the back room for a breath of fresh air.' The timeline also chronicled minor events like the painting of the 'Rent A Cat' sign by an eight-year-old in 2012, with a footnote: 'It's a joke, people'.

The bookshop's website documented the history of its birth: 'In the spring of 2002, Oliver and Craig spent a week on the island of Santorini. The land inspired them and there was no bookshop, so they drank some wine and decided to open one. Oliver named it Atlantis Books and the two laughed about how their children would run it someday.'

I didn't buy any books. They would have been heavy, and I couldn't bear it if the remaining handle on my suitcase broke. Even though I'd dropped some coins in the photography bowl, I was conscious of crowding the little shop as I snapped my shots, and I left before I felt ready.

One of my few regrets on leaving Greece would be that I hadn't perused the wares at Atlantis Books for a little longer, hadn't at least bought a book bag to support them. It's only a tiny qualm, but there it is.

~ ~ ~

Fotini's best advice was to avoid Oia in the evening, when it would be crowded with tourists on their quest for an iconic photograph of a Santorini sunset. She suggested an alternative: Santo Wines, a collective near Pyrgos. I set out by bus and dawdled a few pleasant hours there, joining a tour of the wine cellars, browsing the shop, and then sitting out on the airy terrace to admire the scenery from this different point on the caldera. If Oia was at the top of the crescent-shaped island and Fira a third of the way down, then Santo Wines was two-thirds of the way to its southern tip.

Because I had time to kill, I applied some of it to people watching. Santorini weddings are A Thing, and a celebration was taking place a short distance from where I sat. It was too far away to make out faces, but close enough to appreciate the colourful wedding finery. Just as we were summoned to the cellars, a helicopter landed to whisk the bride and groom to their honeymoon. Our guide was beside herself with excitement. She'd been working there for months, and it was the first time she'd seen a chopper on the helipad.

Her enthusiasm was infectious, and the talk was entertaining, but I've been on lots of wine cellar tours. What caught my attention was not the winemaking processes and paraphernalia but, instead, how the climate of this arid, wind-battered island affected farming methods.

I'm used to seeing vines growing proud and tall, but on Santorini they grow twisted into circular bowl shapes, looking for all the world like birds' nests. This is so they can lie flat, hugging the ground, sheltered from the worst of the island's fierce winds. And, although Santorini has low annual rainfall, the vines don't require artificial irrigation. The volcanic soil acts like a sponge, absorbing moisture from the air during humid weather. This is enough to give the grapes the water they need to survive and thrive.

After the tour, you can choose a tasting flight of six, twelve or eighteen different wines. I opted for a modest serving of six, and a tray of wine samples arrived. It was an attractive presentation with portions of cheese, local tomato and fava pastes garnished with wild capers, delectable seed-encrusted barley rusks and, yes, olives. Pacing myself, it was enough food for the evening.

Earlier, in Oia, I'd eaten in a restaurant that was close to empty when I arrived but filling with sightseers by the time I left. I ordered the *païdakia* I had sought in Meteora, and which featured on the English side of the menu as 'Special Lamp ribs'. It was an adequate lunch, but it wasn't all that well prepared. The contrast with this appetising supper reinforced an oft-observed truth: in general, you need to get away from the most crowded vacation areas to find a memorable meal.

While I was nibbling and sipping, leafing through my book as I waited for sunset, one of the waiters came over to chat. His English was pretty good, but not fluent. He also had a prominent stutter.

At first, I was simply impressed he would strike up a conversation with a stranger in his second language, despite the speech impairment. Even as we chatted, I was questioning my own initial reaction, recognising it could be construed as patronising. It was his easy self-confidence that had struck me, I realised. You see, I often want to try my reasonably-good-but-rusty Afrikaans or not-nearly-as-good-and-even-rustier Spanish, but I lose courage before I can coax the words from my mouth. I rehearse the phrases in Spanish, for example, but they come out in English after all. I am more likely to try my few polite expressions in French, Arabic and, now, Greek. Knowing there is no depth of vocabulary behind these phrases, no prospect of them leading to anything remotely approaching a conversation that might challenge my introversion, I feel safer giving them a go. *But why shouldn't he be more confident than me? Lots of people are. And his English is at least as good as my second language.*

After a while, I stopped over-analysing the waiter's confidence compared to my lack of it, stopped focusing on his stammer. He was an interesting guy and I enjoyed our talk. He asked where I'd travelled in Greece and said I was the first tourist he'd met who had been to Monemvasia and Meteora before coming to Santorini. I'd picked up that Santorini attracts the fashionable party crowd, so this was not as surprising as it might seem. But, when he told me how he'd read up on Monemvasia and watched a captivating documentary about Meteora, and how he longed to visit those places himself, I realised again how lucky I was. I asked about Greece's economy, and he said it was not as healthy as it had been ten years earlier, before the government debt crisis and the resultant austerity packages. 'But better than it was two years ago. Things are improving,' he said, 'but they have a long way to go.'

It wasn't likely he'd be setting off on his own adventures any time soon.

I thought about what it means to be Greek in a time of austerity and what it is to be South African, my nationality by birth and on one of my two passports. There are Greek islanders who have never had the chance to travel outside Greece and seldom leave their own group of islands. At my age, my mother had only been overseas twice, but she was more travelled than most in her social circle. International holidays were less common everywhere in the seventies, but even today, for more privileged middle-class South Africans, global tourism is achievable but not simple. Crossing borders on a South African passport can be a bureaucratic nightmare, while, for an Australian, it is usually a breeze. Paid leave, too, is much more generous in Australia. Planning this holiday from South Africa might have involved years of saving both money and time, but I'd flown to Greece on a whim, knowing that, with my frugality and my salary coming in each week, I would earn almost as much while away as I'd spend. The airfare had been a significant expense, but a couple of months of saving would recoup my costs.

Of course, for the majority of South Africans, a trip like this would be an absolute financial impossibility, something not even to be considered in the daily struggle to make ends meet, even to survive.

Although I have kept my precious South African citizenship and yearn to live again in Cape Town someday – often daydreaming about it and plotting complicated strategies of how to make it happen – I am grateful for the opportunity to travel the world as an Aussie, and for the way Australians have welcomed me to live in their remarkable country. As I confront my own privilege, I am uncomfortably conscious that this welcome isn't extended to everyone. The White Australia policy may have ended half a century ago, but in this era of casual racism and offshore detention camps, it still seems far easier for some people to enter the country than others.

An awareness of my own luck was growing. As was, I admit, a secret pride that this intelligent young man had given my choice of destinations his seal of approval. He'd recognised me as an individual within the mass of tourists on Santorini, and I felt a bit smug about this as the luminous disc of the sun slipped smoothly, and surprisingly swiftly, into the sea.

# CHAPTER FIFTEEN
## SOLO ON SANTORINI

KROTIRI IS LOCATED ON the southern arm of Santorini's main island of Thira, where the base of the crescent starts its curve to the west. It is close to a series of beaches, named after the vivid colours of their sands, that evoke Plato's description of Atlantis: Black Beach, White Beach and Red Beach.

It was once a bustling human settlement. Now, it is just a thought-provoking set of ruins.

In the seventeenth-century BCE, at its peak, Akrotiri was a densely populated town with refined art, multi-storey buildings, and indoor toilets with complex sewerage networks. We know from its wealth of artefacts that it was an affluent community. Plentiful pithoi – large storage jars, some too heavy for a single person to carry – suggest an abundance of food. Sophisticated artworks, portraying exotic creatures like monkeys, hint at a cosmopolitan society with extensive trade and travel networks.

What makes Akrotiri extra special, from an archaeological perspective, is that a thick blanket of debris covered the site during the Minoan eruption. As at better-known Pompeii, this protected the town's buildings and their contents, suspended in a moment as if in amber. Unlike Pompeii, archaeologists have unearthed no mortal remains of people who died during this island-shattering event.

It's like the *Mary Celeste*, but on a much larger scale: an entire population vanished just before natural disaster hit.

A prevailing theory, backed up by signs of damage from *before* the settlement's preservation under layers of volcanic matter, is that a colossal earthquake devastated the city mere weeks before the eruption. This may have caused the inhabitants to flee, either to parts of the island that have not yet been excavated or by boat to Crete. The Cretans would not have been completely surprised by the refugees' arrival; they, too, suffered earthquakes and great falls of ash from Strogili.

~ ~ ~

Before heading out of town, I paid a morning visit to the Museum of Prehistoric Thira. Here, I built on what I'd learned in Athens about Akrotiri's Minoan culture, examining hundreds of well-presented artefacts, most of them from the seventeenth century BCE.

The plaster casts of furniture were particularly evocative. Metres-deep ash and pumice settled over Akrotiri at the time of the eruption. When the town's timber home furnishings eventually crumbled away to nothing, cavities the exact shape of each item remained. Archaeologists filled these moulds with plaster, casting detailed replicas of the originals. In a glass case stood an ornate table that would have felt quite at home in my grandmother's flat.

A figurine of a type of wild goat called an ibex is the only golden object found to have been left behind by Akrotiri's townspeople in the rush from their doomed city. The ibex is the acknowledged star of the collection, but it was the wall paintings that drew me in.

In Athens, I'd come across some of the Akrotiri murals, including a famous painting titled *The Boxing Boys*. Here, in Santorini's museum, stood the *Blue Monkeys* fresco, the *House of the Ladies* frescoes – named for the women in the paintings and not because there is any evidence of it being a house of negotiable affection, as author Terry Pratchett might have put it – and many others. My brief introduction to Minoan mural art had taught me a couple of things. One of these was that artists often used pigmentation to convey the biological sex of humans, with the skin of females painted in pale colours and males painted in darker shades. They also tended to portray women fully clothed, while men and boys were often shown nude or semi-nude, sometimes with partially shaven heads.

After swotting up on Akrotiri, I was keen to see it for myself. It was an easy bus ride away and, when I got there, I found that it was a free-entry day. All the ingredients were there for an enjoyable outing. Unfortunately, an unpleasant tour guide spoiled my visit. I'll call him… well, I'd like to call him a lot of things and would, in fact, quite like to identify him by his real name, but I won't. I'll call him Rihardos.

I'll be the first to admit I don't know a great deal about Minoan art and culture, but even I could tell that Rihardos was talking a load of bull. He spouted some bizarre ideas, contradicting what I'd read and heard in the museums I'd visited over the last three weeks. He didn't present them as hypotheses, though, but as unchallenged truth. Patronising and obviously bored with the effort of speaking to our group, he trotted out one outlandish statement after another.

Pulling out photographs of the frescoes I'd seen in the flesh, as it were, he pointed at images of the women from the *House of the Ladies*. 'Look,' he said, his finger grazing their pale skin, 'Akrotiri was the first Caucasian society. And see the beautiful clothes they are wearing? You cannot work in such outfits.

'Now look at this.' He whipped out a picture of another fresco, this one depicting a man holding up a heavy catch of fish. 'Look at him! He's naked. And look at his dark skin. He is a slave.' His lip curled in a sneer. 'He doesn't even have clothes.'

This was proof, Rihardos told us, that Akrotiri was the first matriarchal society. The women were wealthy, white, powerful and idle. The men had no clothes, they did the work, and they were dark-skinned. Ergo, they were slaves.

*What the…?*

He wasn't finished. Out came a photo of *The Boxing Boys*, the mural I'd seen in Athens. 'Have you been to Olympia? The place of the Ancient Olympics?' he asked. Several people nodded.

'There, they tell you women were not allowed to compete in sports in ancient times. But see, here in Akrotiri, we have proof that girls were boxing. We know they are girls,' he said, 'because of their long hair.'

Okay, I'll grant him that the boys in the painting do appear notably feminine. But the artist painted them in dark pigment, and they are nearly naked, with partially shaven heads showing a faint five o'clock shadow around their longer locks. They're called *The Boxing Boys* for more than one reason.

I'd be intrigued by female boxers or gender fluidity as alternative theories, but he neglected to mention any possibility of them being boys. He was emphatic that they were girls, and that this proved females were athletes on this island long before they were permitted to compete on the mainland. Thus, it followed that Akrotiri was a matriarchal society dominated by wealthy women.

His leaps in logic were dizzying, but he wasn't the first sensationalist or misinformed guide I've met, and he won't be the last. If it weren't for his mocking tone, the arrogance of his talk might even have been entertaining. But I'd been feeling as if he'd kicked me in the gut since before the tour started.

As I'd been first in the queue that morning, I'd had to wait with Rihardos for enough paying visitors to make the tour worth his while. That's when he spotted the bruises on my arms.

My friends and family know how uncoordinated I am. They're used to all four of my limbs displaying patterns of green and blue, the evidence of my clumsiness. I've become so used to daily knocks and bumps that I seldom notice the traces they leave on my body.

Rihardos noticed, though. He said, three times, that if I were *his* woman and came home 'with such bruises, I will give you worse bruises.' His tone was aggressive; even his stance felt predatory. The meaning was clear, and there were at least five layers of ugly in it.

The ugliness streaked through his immediate association of bruises with sex, his assumption that I was unfaithful to Adam, his thinking he had a right to comment on my life. The obscenity of his advocating punitive domestic violence in any situation at all, let alone for the innocent marks I carried, eclipsed the filth of his imagining I could be 'his woman', even hypothetically. I felt physically ill at the threat lurking behind his words and ashamed for not being assertive enough to call him out, or simply to walk away.

A female staff member joined us in a gesture of solidarity that many women will recognise. Her attempts to defuse his remarks were awkward but appreciated, and when she said, 'He is joking,' I meant him to hear my reply, that he wasn't as funny as he thought he was.

'I am not trying to be funny,' he said, quick to insert himself into the exchange.

Rihardos and his foul smirk were the low point of this otherwise wonderful holiday. It took a couple of days before I felt able to talk about what happened with a few female friends online. Our discussion raised the question of whether my perplexing hesitancy to stand up for myself was a symptom of female enculturation that women should throw off. Or whether it was a valid self-preservation tactic in scenarios that, too many of us know from experience, might spiral into violence.

~ ~ ~

Rihardos aside, Akrotiri was awe-inspiring. After he finished his spiel, I went exploring on my own. When I eavesdropped on other guides to see if they were spreading the same bilge, their versions of life at Akrotiri sounded much more informed. I had just drawn the rotten apple from the barrel.

Although the malice in this encounter would be a sour spot in my mind for weeks, I did my best to reset and find adventure in what was left of the day. Wandering the site, I snapped shots of grinding stones, bathtubs, and elegant earthenware pithoi. One of the photographs was of a cracked flight of stone steps, an indication of possible pre-eruption earthquake damage. This could have been the warning that sent the citizens of Akrotiri fleeing for safety.

My professional background in heritage management had me looking beyond the artefacts to the design of the structure. The raised walkways gave access to view a thousand nooks and crannies without any danger to the ancient remains, and the massive roof protected both site and visitors from sunshine or rain. It was, in fact, the second such roof. The original collapsed in 2005, killing one tourist, injuring another six and resulting in the closure of the excavations for several years. I couldn't find any information about whether there were islanders hurt in the incident.

Having had my fill of ancient ruins, I headed on foot to the present-day village of Akrotiri. It boasts a small castle from the period of Venetian occupation, with a thirteenth-century tower called La Ponta, but following the signs to the 'Venetian Castle' through the steep, winding streets led me away from the stronghold, not towards it. When at last I got to the tower, thanks to directions from a local resident, what did I find inside? An exhibition of Greek bagpipes, of all things.

Back at Folia, I tugged off my dusty hiking boots, smelly socks and the underwired bra that had begun to poke me in the side. I switched on the air conditioner and collapsed onto the bed. There is a special kind of tired your legs get after walking on cobblestones, and the exertions of every day on my feet since arriving in Greece had caught up with me. I took two hours off from being a traveller to rest in the calm of my bedroom, away from the crowds, and regather my strength. Fotini had made a 6.30 p.m. reservation for me for sundowner cocktails at Palia Kameni, a fancy cocktail bar named after one of the little islands at the centre of the archipelago. I'd have to get there on time, as there was no chance the sun would delay its performance for me.

When I got to Palia Kameni and saw my table perched on the caldera edge, complete with dainty wrought-iron chairs and a single rose, I knew this would be a good end to an imperfect day. Later that night, I posted a picture of the place setting, my shawl draped over the back of the chair, and the sinking sun blazing a light trail across the ocean far below:

25 September 2016
This one is for Ruby and Megan:
Megan, you would love Santorini. Tonight, I had both a mojito and a Bombay Sapphire gin and tonic in your honour. I miss you and wish you were here with me.

Ruby, gods* help me. I'm back at Folia and I am about to go and have the home-cooked dinner your mother-in-law has saved for me. And I am on the far side of tipsy. I'd swear that G&T was a quadruple shot!

*Grecian gods, of course.

# CHAPTER SIXTEEN
## SANTORINI TO RHODES

To get to Fira's old port, I had to clamber down six hundred steps. There'd be no donkey rides for me. I'd read many of these animals are poorly treated, and I had no desire to add my weight to their troubles.

The Minoan eruption left just three islands standing in Santorini's archipelago: Thira, the tiny islet of Aspronisi, and Thirasia, which does its best to complete the circle but doesn't quite succeed. The accumulation of volcanic matter over the millennia resulted in the two central Kameni islands rising from the ocean. Today's boat excursion would take me, and scores of others chatting away in a veritable Babel of languages, to all these, except little Aspronisi.

Our first stop was just off the coast of Palia Kameni – the namesake for the previous night's cocktail bar with the lethal G&Ts – where thermal springs showed as a deepening pool of yellow in the water near the island. The springs were a symptom of ongoing volcanic activity, and the sulphur and iron in the water caused its rich hue. I'd been warned twice not to wear white when swimming here, as the mineral-laden seawater would discolour the fabric.

The boat stopped some distance from shore, and the highlight of my day was beating my fear of heights to cannonball into the cold seawater. Flinging myself from the deck was a gesture against the inevitable creep of middle age I'd make while I still could. I may have passed my own midlife milestone, but no way was I going down the ladder with the rest of the oldies. Not yet, anyway.

The next stop was Nea Kameni, the site of the volcanic cone, where we trudged up the black sand to the lip of its crater. Heat emanated from the dark, shingle-strewn powder, and I was one of the last from our boat to get to the summit, making a mockery of my earlier exuberant stab at youth. It was worth the hard slog, though; the views were spectacular. The islands around us cupped a giant bowl of blue, and the clifftop cascade of white dwellings brought to mind a dusting of icing sugar. Even the monolithic cruise ship anchored off Thira seemed less jarring from this height.

Turning back to the dry earth of Nea Kameni, I gazed at the triviality of hats blown into the crater by the gusting wind and wondered if anyone else was thinking my thoughts: *The cycle that destroys and rebuilds these islands hasn't stopped.* Lava last flowed here in 1950, but magma is still boiling deep in the Earth's core. It is certain to force its way to the surface again, spewing molten rock into the steaming sea and a thick plume of black debris into the air. *One day, a layer of ash will settle on the rim of the caldera, replacing those pretty, white buildings. It could be in ten thousand years, or it might be next week. Who knows?*

Our last stop was the only other inhabited land of the archipelago. Thirasia could offer an interesting glimpse into what Thira was like before the tourism boom catapulted the larger island into commercialism. But when we got there, I was famished. Instead of climbing the many steps to the clifftop village, I set out along the waterfront to the furthest taverna. Picking my way past the various eateries, I found myself missing Adam, Carly and Megan. My partner, niece and best friend were all lovers of seafood. The last time the four of us were together, they'd feasted on shellfish on a South African beach, while I made do with cheese and day-old bread at a safe distance. If they'd been here, they'd have been in tentacle heaven. With my aversion to seafood, though, the ingredients on display were a *Pirates of the Caribbean* nightmare of suckers and claws.

I asked for a vegetarian platter in my best pidgin Greek. While I waited, a playful kitten batted at my shawl as it fluttered in a salt-tinged breeze. The meal turned out to be a tasteless capsicum and rice dish accompanied by limp salad and stale chips, but the atmosphere was a balm to my frazzled nerves after the ugliness that had marred my visit to Akrotiri.

I was having a lovely last day on Santorini, and there was more fun in store.

On my clifftop walk to Oia two days before, I'd spotted a poster for outdoor movies at the Volkan Cinema Festival. Even Fotini hadn't heard of these screenings, so we decided to see a film together on my final night on the island. Last-minute work demands prevented her from joining me – wedding planning is not as easy as you might think – and I headed off to the caldera edge alone.

I had to restrain myself from singing along while *Mamma Mia!* blazed from the big screen. This feel-good musical was set on a fictional Greek isle named Kalokairi and shot on the real Greek island of Skopelos, and there was something magical about watching it out under the stars. Instead of contributing my off-key melodies to the soundtrack, I sipped a margarita and dined on a selection of breads, local cheeses, sweet baby peppers stuffed with feta, wild capers and cherry tomatoes.

There's nothing like a hefty dose of ABBA and over-the-top choreography to lift your spirits. It's a pity Fotini couldn't make it. It would have made a great girls' night out.

~ ~ ~

My four-night stay on Santorini had come to an end, and the bus schedule gave me two choices: to get to the airport either three hours before my flight or one hour beforehand. I'd heard the departures terminal could be chaotic at times, so I took the early shuttle. The practicalities of identifying the correct vehicle and loading my luggage pushed any fear of bus travel from my mind.

The airport check-in queue stalled as a couple of emaciated, leathery sun-worshippers, dripping with bling but lacking in respect, swore at a member of the airline ground crew. She had informed them it was too soon to check in for their flight, and they gave her an earbashing before dragging their weighty baggage away, grumbling obscenities.

Behind them, the woman's face crumpled for just a moment. Then, smooth mask of professionalism back in place, she turned to me, the next in line. I stepped up to her desk with my brightest smile and thanked her in Greek when she gave me the same information.

Finding a rare vacant seat, I settled in to wait, but sometimes there is an unexpected payoff for treating others with common decency. It was only minutes later that an airline official sought me out and offered me an earlier flight. My connection from Athens to Rhodes would still leave at the same time, but my wait would be in a spacious international airport with free Wi-Fi, comfortable seats, and my luggage already checked all the way through. It did mean I had to race to Santorini's boarding gate and then wait until our plane landed in the capital before I could scrabble through my backpack's pockets to locate my breakfast: a light, sugary doughnut purchased that morning from Svoronos. This excellent twenty-four-hour bakery was two minutes' walk from Folia, so I'd been a frequent customer, and I was missing it before I'd swallowed the last bite.

~ ~ ~

Rhodes was my final port of call, and I had mixed feelings about how to organise my time there. I'd originally planned for five nights on the island, which would have made it my longest stay apart from the writers' retreat. When my itinerary changed to accommodate the extra days needed to visit Meteora, though, I had to cut that time from somewhere. After a Tetris-like spreadsheet exercise of arranging destinations and transport options in a variety of patterns, I sliced it from my stay on Rhodes.

This meant I was now about to land on an island I didn't have nearly enough time to explore.

I approach every destination with a loose list of landmarks to visit. There might be a few absolute must-dos, but, in general, I tend to gather suggestions from friends, TripAdvisor and my *Lonely Planet*, and then let my moods and interests guide what I do each day. If something unexpected piques my curiosity, I shed my plans in an instant, always happiest when 'following my nose'.

But Rhodes is a large island, with much to see, so there was some pressure to plan out my activities. Research had narrowed my shortlist to three sites, but each of these could consume a full day with ease. Plus, two of them required hours of travel set to inconvenient public transport schedules.

The candidates were:

Lindos, a superb example of the archetypical whitewashed Grecian village. It has an ancient acropolis, blue lagoon and handsome views.

Rhodes Old Town, a medieval walled town inscribed on the World Heritage List. The town dates in part to the epoch of the Crusades and its occupation by the Knights of Saint John, the same order that went on to settle in Malta after their sixteenth-century defeat by the Ottoman Empire. It includes both Turkish and Jewish quarters and plenty of museums and historical buildings, although much of its charm lies in simply wandering its twisting alleyways.

Symi, a mountainous island close to the Turkish mainland and just a ferry ride away from Rhodes. Symi has a harbour surrounded by neoclassical buildings in a palette of pastels, which I'd been told is unforgettably beautiful, as well as a monastery said to contain a miraculous icon of the Archangel Michael.

The only way I could fit them all in was to spend three quarters of a day each at Lindos and Symi, and try to squeeze a couple of hours in the Old Town into the early mornings and evenings. It was going to be tight. Extremely tight.

Via email, I'd asked the owner of my Rhodes hotel for advice in solving this dilemma. He was helpful, describing the drawcards of each site and sending me bus and ferry timetables. He did, however, include an important caveat: 'Although Rhodes has to offer a lot, you should relax, use all of your senses and enjoy your adventure in Greece.'

~ ~ ~

By the time I arrived at the hotel, conveniently located on the bus route from the airport to Rhodes Town, it had been a long day since my bakery breakfast. The owner – let's call him Vasilis – greeted me with the offer of a glass of ouzo. All I wanted, though, was to wash away the travel grime, find something to eat and go to sleep. I politely turned down the welcome drink.

After a quick shower, I headed across the road to a restaurant where the jovial waiter brought a complimentary bowl of olives to my table with the menu. I tucked into them with gusto.

# CHAPTER SEVENTEEN
## RHODES ROAMINGS

T HE PALE LIGHT OF morning glowed through my eyelids but, for a moment, I couldn't bring myself to open them. I yearned for just one lazy day: a day of reading, napping and playing word games on my phone to recuperate before heading back out to discover the world. I wasn't ready for my adventure to end, but all the fabulousness was taking its toll. With only two days to explore Rhodes, though, I hadn't yet worked out how to fit everything in. I had to get up, get my *kefi* back and get going.

It was early by Greek standards, with most attractions still closed, so I had some leeway to set out on foot. Attempting to get to the beachfront, I soon found myself inadvertently trespassing through a glossy resort, complete with the cornflower blue of a deserted infinity pool gleaming against the deeper azure of the sea. Private hotels lined the beach, so I'd have to walk beside the noisy road, with convoys of coaches labelled 'Lindos' thundering by in the opposite direction.

The commute took longer than expected, and I couldn't help but feel anxious at how time was speeding away. There were several bus stops on my route, and I checked the timetable at each as I went. At one stop, with a bus due any moment, I decided to take the quicker option into Rhodes Town. But the bus didn't arrive on schedule, and, after ten minutes of waiting, my impatience got the better of me. Predictably, it pulled up next to the other, more patient passengers not two minutes after I left. A wave of disgruntlement swept through me, but it was only a few moments later that I found a cheerful bakery breakfast I could munch as I walked.

As if in response to my lighter mood, the oceanfront road peeled away from the main drag, leaving the clamorous traffic and general unattractiveness behind. It ran between a stretch of dilapidated cottages backing onto scrub-covered hills on one side, and a drop to the sea on the other. This was a welcome respite from the concrete jungle I'd left behind, and I wondered how long the area would hold its own before development encroached.

To my left, an unexpected pathway curved down to the water. It led to a well-maintained footpath, of packed sand between low stone walls, that continued the whole way to Rhodes Town. Foaming surf surged around rocks in a soothing murmur; even the shrill squawk of a gull overhead rang with jubilant freedom. The road had disappeared from view and my spirits soared as I drank in the sensuality of salt in the air, focusing on the calming repetition of placing one foot in front of the other.

When I got to Rhodes Town, I abandoned the shortcut I'd mapped through city streets. Instead, I continued along the ocean path to the northernmost tip of the island. Passing the tiny Art Deco building housing the aquarium, I crunched out onto the beach and, crouching, dipped my hand into the water. Across the sea stood the landmass of Turkey, a country visited by my great-great-grandmother in an era when some regions of Greece were still part of the declining Ottoman Empire. Now, it lay within tantalising sight, just forty kilometres away. *This water cupped in my hand,* I wondered, *does it belong to the Aegean or the Mediterranean Sea?*

In need of rejuvenation, I stopped for fresh orange juice at a roadside stall. As the sweet nectar slipped down my throat, a deserted minaret drew my eyes across a busy street. Its silent call reverberated with the beat of my heart. My feet followed my eyes, until I could peer through metal palings at an evocative forest of old tombstones engraved with Arabic-like Ottoman script. I had learned the Arabic alphabet years before when I lived in Abu Dhabi, but I couldn't recall anything other than how to scrawl my own name in childish letters. I was unable to make out a single word on the stones. This was a pity, as I have occupied many fascinating hours wandering historical graveyards around the world, deciphering the inscriptions and imagining the lifetimes of the people buried there.

There was no visible entrance to the cemetery from where I stood, so I followed the fence around its perimeter. As I rounded a corner, I happened upon a yellow cottage with a plaque on its wall: 'In this house lived the philhellene and friend of Rhodes, poet and novelist Lawrence G. Durrell, from 20-5-1945 to 10-4-1947.'

I'd heard of Lawrence's work but never read it; I only knew him as a character in Gerald Durrell's childhood memoirs, a trilogy beginning with *My Family and Other Animals*. When I'd put out that call to my friends for suggestions of books set in Greece, it was this title that popped up, again and again. My father had loved *The Corfu Trilogy*, but when I'd pulled it from his bookshelves as a teenager, it didn't hold my attention.

Lawrence was Gerald's big brother, and, standing at his doorstep, I resolved to find the elder Durrell's novels on my return to Australia. When I later borrowed one from the library, though, I found it pretentious. Both brothers won literary acclaim, and Gerald inspired a love for travel and the natural world in many young readers. Somehow, though, I just couldn't get into either author's work. Still, Lawrence was the embodiment of the bohemian set that swung through Europe between the two World Wars. And he was a philhellene – a friend of Greece – in the trend of writers from Lord Byron to Australian Nobel Laureate

Patrick White, all the way to Tom Hanks who, while better known as an actor, has published a volume of thoughtful short stories titled *Uncommon Type*. It was a quiet thrill to stumble upon the elder Durrell's home.

My library didn't have a copy of Lawrence's book *The Greek Islands*, but an online search brought up this quote about the time he lived in a house called Villa Cleobolus:

> It was in Rhodes where I spent such happy post-war years, locked into the sacred garden of Murat Reis. I was indeed living in a Turkish cemetery of such beauty and silence that I often longed to die and be sealed into one of those beautiful forms; to lie there dreaming for ever of Eyoub and the great ladies who dream away time in the vehement silence of the Turkish heat, with just the sound of the leaves falling…

I had almost completed my circuit around the edge of the property before an open gate beckoned me inside. The sixteenth-century mosque looked as if it had been shut up for many years, but the 'sacred garden' welcomed me. I wandered the graves, wondered about the inhabitants of the mausoleums and, leaving my footwear alongside a few pairs of traditional wooden bath sandals at the door, entered a small prayer room to pay my respects to those laid to rest here.

The room had modern furnishings and an air of regular use. Hanging from a green curtain was a ribbon-tied cluster of *tamata*. Each *tama* is a small tin plate embossed with a symbolic image: babies for those praying for fertility, or parts of the body for those seeking relief from injury or disease. These were the same offerings that decorate Christian churches throughout Greece.

I'd walked ten kilometres, and the morning was ebbing away. I hadn't even made it as far as the Old Town, and I was already falling in love with Rhodes. The anxiety over managing my day had dissipated with the water that slid from my fingers at the beach, and my unhurried stroll through the grounds of the mosque had calmed me. I would devote the day to Rhodes Town, taking my time to explore both the 'new' and old towns at a leisurely pace. Tonight, I'd decide whether it would be Lindos or Symi that would make the cut for tomorrow.

Lindos, particularly, was beginning to seem more of an obligation than a pleasure. So many people had recommended I go there, and I would have liked to see it. But I had visited plenty of ruined Grecian temples and blue-and-white villages over the past few weeks, and the number of coaches heading there led me to suspect it would be packed with tourists. Symi, with its proximity to Turkey and its promise of a never-to-be-forgotten view of its pretty harbour, was the more likely contender.

For now, I'd head to nearby Mandraki Harbour, the alleged site of the Colossus of Rhodes, one of the Seven Wonders of the Ancient World. Popular legend has it that this third-century BCE statue of Helios, the sun god, straddled the waterway and was so enormous that tall ships' masts could sail between his towering legs. Engineering practicalities suggest this was an improbable location, but the image is an arresting one.

Helios was brought low by an earthquake after a century on guard duty. Today, a much more modest stag marks the harbour entrance on one side, while a doe stands on the other, exactly where I'd like to imagine Helios's great feet once rested. Christina, the receptionist at Doupiani House in Meteora, told me she had studied on Rhodes and that she and her fellow students had often met up at these statues of deer. She asked me to send her a picture of them when I got here, so I took one of my few selfies of the trip to email to her later.

By now, my bladder was complaining. And I'd forgotten I would need a fifty-cent piece to unlock the public loos. I shouldn't have frittered away my small change on that orange juice. As I scanned the busy waterfront, I spotted something a little different: among the many vendors and touts was one spruiking a ride in a 'glass-bottomed semi-submarine'. It even had a bathroom onboard. Instead of spending fifty cents on a toilet – which I had yet to locate and for which I had no coins – I could hand over a ten-euro note for a forty-five-minute boat ride under the ghost of Helios's legs and around the harbour, with the opportunity to go down into the windowed hold and watch fish flock to where a diver was releasing food into the water. It didn't occur to me to consider the ecological impacts of this practice. I've no idea whether it was harmful, but I have an uneasy suspicion that it may have been. The use of food to attract wildlife to humans so often is.

Nevertheless, it was from this boat that I caught my first glimpses of the Old Town. After disembarking and buying a lukewarm ear of corn from a roadside stallholder, who was using a hand-held hairdryer to whip some life into the dying embers of her barbecue, I made my way to the Crusader walls at last.

Although I had an entire afternoon to wander, my plans derailed, and I saw only the tiniest part of the medieval town that day. I entered through the imposing Liberty Gate, briefly visited the small municipal art gallery, and paused at the ruined third-century BCE Temple of Aphrodite. Then I headed into the archaeological museum housed in the fifteenth-century stronghold of the Knights Hospitaller Order of Saint John. And that's where I stayed.

Through hall after hall, examining marvel after marvel, I meandered for hours. It was soon clear I'd be dedicating the rest of this day not only to the artefacts displayed, but also to the moods evoked while wandering through the courtyards, staircases, passageways and chambers of this massive building in which the Crusaders worked, slept and ate. In which they breathed.

Covering Classical, Hellenistic, Roman, Early Christian, Medieval and Ottoman periods, the exhibits included ancient burial finds and knights' funerary slabs, pottery and statuary, mosaics and jewellery. Across a small courtyard sat a building restored to the simple style of a nineteenth-century Ottoman home. Through the wild gardens stood an exhibition of detailed reconstructions of archaeological digs, including the burial of a seventeenth-century BCE warrior laid to rest with his horse.

Among the statues scattered throughout the museum were two graceful sculptures of Aphrodite, the Grecian goddess of love, beauty and procreation. One, possibly the cult statue from the ruined temple I'd seen a few hours earlier, had endured an undisclosed period on the seabed. This had caused a bit of damage to her nether regions. A label on the pedestal explained, 'The erosion of the sculpture in the sea enhances the fluidity of its original volumes and planes.'

My thoughts, posted on social media with a photo of her dimpled behind?

28 September 2016

Leave her lying around in the sea long enough,
and even Aphrodite will get cellulite.

~ ~ ~

Still on a high when I arrived back at the hotel, I bubbled over
with enthusiasm when Vasilis asked about my day. I skipped
up the steps to my room to take a shower, change for dinner,
and break the news to my friends online: I'd made up my
mind. No Lindos, and no Symi, either.

Instead of cramming as many places as possible into my
trip, I'd slow down. I'd appreciate what I had, rather than
always chasing after more. There was the local acropolis to
visit, and then I'd delve further into the Old Town, seeing
if I could locate Greece's oldest active synagogue and, as
always, the hammam.

# CHAPTER EIGHTEEN
## WRAPPING UP IN RHODES

COOL CELLOPHANE CRINKLED BENEATH my fingertips as I rummaged around in my suitcase looking, without much hope, for something clean to wear. It was the Grecian dress I'd bought in an Athens souvenir shop, still in its wrapper, and I decided to frock up. After all, I'd carted make-up and jewellery halfway around the world and hadn't used any of it. I pulled the turquoise dress over my head, slapped on some mascara, eyeliner and a touch of lipstick, and slipped on a necklace and bracelet.

On my way past the reception desk, Vasilis renewed last night's offer of a complimentary drink. Far too hungry to delay dinner – the tepid corn hadn't done much for me – I agreed to an ouzo later, when I got back from the nearby taverna he had recommended.

And, oh, what a brilliant find it was! Aptly named 'Mama's', it was a family-run taverna with Mama in the kitchen, son at the souvlaki grill and daughter waiting the tables. How often do you have your waitress come out while you're eating your salad to tell you, 'I'm sorry, but your meatballs aren't ready yet. My mother wasn't satisfied with the first batch, so she threw them away and started again'?

It was early for a Greek dinner and I was the only customer, so Eleni and I were able to chat while we waited for the main course. We talked about the taverna and she told me that Mama was a perfectionist who allowed her two sons to cook in the restaurant, but never her daughter. We discussed basil in churches and the Trump-Clinton presidential campaign. When she remarked that my outfit was pretty, I apologised for how touristy it was. She disagreed. 'My mother has a dress like that, just a different colour,' she said.

Given that I'd assumed I was closer in age to Eleni than her mother, this robbed me of a little of my pleasure in her praise.

Eleni asked for my phone to take a picture. Posting the photo on social media, I described how her mother threw out my meatballs. As an afterthought, I explained how Eleni insisted I pose in profile to hide that I had, with typical inelegance, drizzled salad dressing down my front.

Among the many comments was one from Ruby's brother Tasso, my pre-teen crush. He's a Facebook acquaintance, but we hadn't had any direct communication for many years. Presumably alluding to the dramatic gesture by the charismatic Mama, he remarked, 'That can only happen in Greece.'

'Oh no,' I quipped. 'I disagree. I can spill salad dressing on a brand-new garment just about anywhere.'

I'm such a prize. Ha! I bet he's sorry now he didn't hold on to me when he had the chance.

After polishing off Mama's cherry spoon sweets, a mouth-watering dessert of fruit and yoghurt, I headed back to the hotel. Vasilis had set out a table on the front terrace with two chairs, two glasses, a bottle of ouzo, a pitcher of water and dishes of olives and cheese. He cracked the seal on the bottle as I approached, and it occurred to me that this might not be a routine welcome drink. I popped upstairs to grab a shawl, a) to hide the aforementioned salad-dressing, but mainly b) because of my sudden realisation that I was – with credit to my book-club friends for the phrase – 'out with the girls'. Just a bit. There wasn't so much cleavage on display that people would stop and stare, but it was more than was appropriate for an evening drink alone with a man who wasn't Adam.

The ouzo clouded our glasses as it reacted to the chilled water, and an agreeable hour followed. Vasilis was an entertaining companion with a wealth of knowledge about the island. He was obviously pleased that I hadn't rushed my visit to Rhodes Town, and it was clear he was enjoying my company. As I was his. We chatted about Greece and Australia and South Africa, and his grandfather who came to Rhodes from Turkey before the population exchange.

The flirtation was subtle at first, but I was on my guard. I'd already mentioned my 'husband' a few times. Adam and I are not actually married, but an explanation of Australian de facto partnerships might have muddled the issue at this point. I was painfully aware of where the line was (in exactly the place where I would feel hurt if Adam were to cross it) and was scrupulous with my words.

But I'll be frank: the temptation was real.

Vasilis was rather dishy with classic Greek features. His conversation was intelligent, varied and witty, and there was something achingly attractive in being desired by someone new. Trying his luck with solo female guests might be his usual practice, but I didn't hold this against him. *Why shouldn't he play the field?* He was maybe a decade younger than me and appeared to be single; he spoke of his daughter with love and her mother with respect. And his approach wasn't threatening, or sleazy. He flattered like a pro, scoring high points for showing interest in my itinerary and, especially, for praising my few phrases of Greek.

When the flirting became more blatant – he said I looked like a Greek goddess in this dress and, seizing on my plans to visit the acropolis the next day, started to tell me how romantic a setting it was – I cut things short and firmly took myself off, alone, to bed. There was a minor earthquake during the night, but I slept through it in the deep slumber of the innocent.

~ ~ ~

On the last full day of my holiday, I navigated through suburban streets to the Rhodes acropolis. This acropolis is neither as large nor as restored as other archaeological sites I'd seen on this trip, but it did include, in addition to its ruined temples and scaffolded columns, a small theatre and an impressive stadium. I strode around the track in the footsteps of athletes of old and then, more fittingly, climbed the tiers to sit on stone seats worn smooth by the posteriors of ancient couch potatoes.

My route to the Old Town took me through a small park set up for children to learn the rules of the road, with narrow, criss-crossing 'streets' and a jumbled scattering of scaled-down road signs. Then there was the brooding statue of a monk outside the San Francisco Catholic Church to contemplate, and the weekly open-air market to browse. But the Old Town was waiting, and I soon crossed the bridge over the moat to Saint John's Gate.

Just inside this gate stood the modest fifteenth-century church of Saint John the Baptist. It was empty of furniture apart from a single unoccupied folding chair, its floor swept clean and the faded remains of its frescoes barely visible. This quiet space seemed, somehow, more atmospheric than the gorgeous, gilded churches I had seen throughout Greece.

I meandered around cobbled alleyways, searching for the Jewish and Turkish quarters of the Old Town. Passing four black garments – two skirts and two blouses – pegged on a clothesline that hugged a crumbling stone wall, I thought to myself, *A widow lives here*. And wondered whether she was the owner of the shiny motor scooter tucked in beneath the laundry.

Then I found the Kahal Shalom Synagogue and its adjoining museum.

The synagogue itself felt open and airy, but there were hints of darkness in the few French phrases I could puzzle out from a plaque affixed to the timber furnishings, commemorating the deaths of the Franco family. The hand-carved letters left no room for the intricacies of accents or punctuation, but its tragic message was clear: '*en memoire des membres de leur famille*', '*et leurs enfants*', and, '*morts en deportation en 1 annee 1944.*'

The museum traces the history of the local Jewish community, starting with the Romaniote Jews who were living here by 1309 and spoke Judeo-Greek. After the Ottomans conquered Rhodes in 1522, Spanish-speaking Sephardic Jews also settled on the island. Sultan Süleyman the Magnificent was known for welcoming Jewish refugees to his empire. He was following a tradition set by his grandfather. In the late fifteenth century, Sultan Bayezid II had taunted the Catholic king Ferdinand for enriching Turkey and its dominions even as he impoverished his own country, when he expelled the Jews from Spain.

For the most part, the exhibits focused on the Jewish way of life through the island's history, showcasing ceremony, costume, and patterns of migration. A small *mikveh*, or ritual bath, sat across from decorated wooden sandals that would have graced the feet of a bride as she bathed before her wedding. They looked very much like the ones I'd seen the day before outside a Muslim prayer room. In an era when so many exploit religion as a difference to be feared, I was soothed by the links and similarities between faiths I found as I moved through Greece.

After walking past displays of dresses and washing bowls, marriage contracts and holy books, historical photographs and portrayals of the celebrations of the living, I came to a small room. Its panels, printed with a silhouette of barbed wire, narrated a harrowing tale told in the voices of the Jewish women of Rhodes, and particularly through the testimony of Holocaust survivor Lucia Capelluto.

It began on 16 July 1944, when the Nazis rounded up the men. The women were ordered to join them two days later:

> Friday and Saturday night, we lay on the floor, anguished and sleepless. As for food, nothing was given to us...
> We had straw and light blankets from which we extracted threads to knit socks using slivers of

wood tored from our bunks. If caught, we would have been charged of sabotaging the property of the Reich…

I slept between Stella with typhus and my sister Rachel who had dysentery, yet I caught nothing. We were calm and resigned to the notion of dying. I had turned 18 in February…

The concentration camps swallowed up at least 1,673 Jewish citizens of Rhodes, although it was likely more. A simple table in German, later forwarded to me by a representative of the Jewish Community of Rhodes, states that the convoy from the island brought *2,500* Greek Jews to the gates of Auschwitz on 16 August 1944, with a footnote explaining that the italics indicate the number is an estimate. Around *1,900* of these men, women and children, were '*vergasten*'.

Gassed.

It is the very vagueness of this italicised estimate (*1,900*), contrasted with the precise counts of prisoners admitted to the male (346) and female (254) areas of the camp, that brings the fearful misery of the scene home to me: the milling confusion tamed into exhausted queues; the terrified hundreds wrenched from their families; the far longer lines – of those deemed disposable – fed into the grey maws of the gas chambers.

I can feel my own mouth twisting as I type the words. In black on white, they're brutal. Of those six hundred human beings funnelled away from the gas chambers and into the camp, only 151 walked free at the end of the war.

There were also two stories of how the Muslim community of Rhodes came to the aid of their Jewish compatriots.

In early 1944, when the synagogue's congregation decided to hide its precious religious documents, the Muslim Grand Mufti of Rhodes took into safekeeping their Sefer Torahs. Şeyh Süleyman Kaşlıoğlu concealed these handwritten scrolls, containing Judaism's holiest text, in the pulpit of the Murat Reis Mosque – the same mosque around which I'd wandered the previous morning. He was confident the Nazis would never suspect this hiding place, and he was correct. After the war, Kaşlıoğlu returned the scrolls, including one of the oldest Sefer Torahs in the world, to the few Jews of Rhodes who survived Auschwitz and Bergen-Belsen.

Then, on 20 July 1944, just before three freight ships transported the imprisoned Jews to the mainland, the Turkish Consul General of Rhodes demanded the release of those who were of Turkish nationality – the only ones he had any power to rescue – as well as their families. The Nazis refused, but Selahattin Ülkümen persisted, bamboozling them with bureaucracy and citing various treaties and agreements until, with reluctance, they let dozens of families go. This almost certainly saved their lives, though the freed Jews were subject to ongoing harassment until they fled to Turkey.

German planes bombed the Turkish Consulate on Rhodes two weeks after Ülkümen secured the release of the Turkish Jews. The attack resulted in the immediate deaths of two staff and the serious wounding of Ülkümen's pregnant wife. She gave birth to their little boy before dying a week later, and, back in Australia, I'd weep as I watched an interview with this surviving son. When Turkey abandoned neutrality, joining forces with the Allies in 1945, Ülkümen himself was incarcerated on mainland Greece until the war ended.

Today, just a handful of Jewish people live on the island of Rhodes. When the exhibition panel was printed, there were thirty-seven. Now, a response to my query tells me, 'We are much less.'

~ ~ ~

I set off in search of the *Hora*, the Old Town's Turkish quarter. Following a tourist map down narrow alleys, guided by landmarks, I soon found the hammam, but its doors were locked. A little further along the winding laneways, I came across the Mosque of Süleyman and the gracefully furnished two-roomed library that Hafiz Ahmed Agha, a high-ranking Ottoman official, established in 1793. Among the documents on display were handwritten pages adorned with flowers painted in delicate watercolours. They were from a medical reference work dated to 1135 in the Islamic calendar, or 1723 in the Common Era.

Hafiz Ahmed Agha was a philanthropist, and as part of his *vakfiye* – a deed of trust or endowment – he made ongoing financial provisions for the payment of library staff, for the distribution of food to the poor, and for twenty dervishes to chant the declaration, 'There is no God but God,' seventy thousand times, on four important religious dates each year. The largest part of his legacy was set aside to purchase the freedom of Muslim slaves held captive on the island of Malta, still governed at that time by the Knights of Saint John who had once occupied Rhodes. Thankfully, the executors had to put this bequest to other uses after the 1833 abolition of slavery during Malta's British occupation.

Even though it was still mid-afternoon, I was ready to wrap up my Greek vacation. I plotted my route to the hotel past the Palace of the Grand Master, the Street of the Knights and, quite by chance, a tiny museum of marine archaeology.

When I saw Vasilis, he invited me to join him for another ouzo. I can't say this was a surprise. Last night's temptation, easily controlled, had simmered through the day into something primal: an urge to allow my tumble into love with Rhodes Town to culminate in a climax of raw desire, separate from everything I held dear.

That wasn't what I needed, though. No matter how spectacular a shattering of midlife mundanity it might make.

While last night had been innocent, sharing a drink this evening would be inviting a seduction I might find hard to resist. Vasilis persisted, but I hid the hot pulse of my attraction with a light laugh, telling him good-naturedly it was impossible that I'd change my mind, and headed upstairs to pack for an early start on the long haul home.

At some point during the evening, a note appeared under my door:

> Even if the time we spent together was very short, the quality and the variety of feelings were very rich.
> With this letter I would like, by expressing just a little bit of my thoughts and feelings, make you understand that Greeks acting with passion, the whole Greek culture is based on this… even if I know that it's almost impossible, I still hope, I guess you know that from history, Greeks are always going for the impossible.

The note ended with his WhatsApp contact details. The digits stared up at me, as alluring as a siren song and just as dangerous. I felt a pang of loss, of mourning for a time when I'd been that delicious combination of young and single, both wanted and wanton. There'd never been a chance that I'd cheat on Adam, but what I would have labelled 'unthinkable' a month earlier had nevertheless slipped its thirsty way into my thoughts. Sleep didn't come quite so smoothly that night, but it came at last.

What did you think? I told you this wasn't going to be a *Shirley Valentine* story.

# CHAPTER NINETEEN
# HEADING HOME: A
# FACEBOOK LOG

30 September 2016

Just over three weeks ago, it took me forty-four hours, two train journeys and four flights to get from my flat to glorious Greece. I've stayed in six places – two island destinations and four on the mainland – and each has been unique. Now it's time for a bus to the airport. Then five flights and a train ride home to Adam.

2 October 2016

I have adventurous luggage. Over the last two days I've been in the airports of Rhodes, Athens, Amsterdam, Kuala Lumpur, Jakarta and now Sydney. My bag, however, has gone to Korea.

3 October 2016

Luggage has arrived. My trip door-to-door took almost fifty hours. My bag took an extra thirteen. Holidays are now officially over. Back to work tomorrow.

20 October 2016

Eating olives. It's just not the same.

# AFTER: REFLECTIONS

## CHAPTER TWENTY
## LOOKING BACK

O<small>N</small> 22 O<small>CTOBER</small> 2016, a year to the day before I typed the first jumbled draft of this chapter, I woke from a vivid dream that I was writing a book about my Greek holiday. Before I'd even rubbed the sleep from my eyes, I shared a jokey Facebook post about the dream. A flood of comments encouraged me to give it a go. The seed of the idea settled for a few weeks, and then, one day, I opened my laptop and began to type.

Limnisa had introduced me to a mind-blowing truth: novelists could start writing a book *without knowing how it was going to end.* Creating fiction is in a whole different league from drafting non-fiction; the ability to invent authentic characters and believable, complex plots is a magic I cannot fathom. And the concept of setting out on that gruelling journey without a map bewilders me.

Sulari Gentill is one of my favourite Australian authors. The first two books of her Hero trilogy – a fantastical young adult reimagining of Homer's *The Iliad* and *The Odyssey* and Virgil's *The Aeneid* – accompanied me on my 2016 expedition through Greece. She's better known for her historical mysteries and metafiction, and I've heard her speak about how her characters can run away with her story. She once announced on social media that, twenty-seven chapters into the novel she was writing, she had only just figured out who the murderer was!

I didn't expect my own manuscript to surprise me. After all, I was preparing a straightforward travelogue: a chronological description of the places I'd visited, and what occurred while I was there. But, as the story evolved, themes burrowed to the surface like fine green shoots.

This was supposed to be a simple 'what I did on my holidays' travel book, framed by my quest to reclaim my travel mojo a decade after the accident in Sri Lanka. It wasn't long before another message wrote itself into the story: you can be an out-of-shape, middle-aged traveller on a budget and still have a life-changing adventure. The trick is taking just a step away from the mass tourism track. That's where I found what I had lost, hidden inside a buried husk of unexplored anxieties.

Enigmatic and often unsatisfying as it was, Mum's travel diary was an obvious inclusion, but the strength of my sisters' presence in this manuscript took me aback. Jenny and Tassin have grown steadily more important to me since our friendship blossomed in Peru, and their voices spoke to me as I wrote. But sisterhood is defined by more than blood. Shauna and Megan are my sisters too. So is Fiona, the mother of my niece Carly who shared my travel ethos like no one else.

Carly once told me her favourite book was *Shantaram* by Gregory David Roberts, a semi-autobiographical work set in India. She described how she'd been captivated by the book's account of informal medicine in a Mumbai slum. Carly grew up to be the other nomad in the family and an ambulance paramedic who saved many lives, but we lost her to a motorcycle accident in Hanoi before I could pester her to read my own travel story. When I write about my small triumphs over fear of road travel, the irony pierces my heart. I should have dedicated this book to Adam – it's not easy living with a writer – but he gets why it is a tribute to my precious barefoot niece.

If you've enjoyed these pages, you probably share my fascination with uncovering morsels of knowledge in each location you visit, whether they be historical, mythical, linguistic, geological or, let's be honest, gastronomic. In one place, it could be the landscape that clutches at my imagination. In another, it might be a glimpse of ritual that intrigues me. It was foreseeable that heritage would become a theme, most noticeably expressed as I explored one World Heritage Site after another.

By contrast, books weren't intended to play such a strong role. It became clear as I wrote, though, that my reading pile was central to my discovery of Greece, both through what these books taught me and because they were my constant companions.

The internet has transformed travel within a single generation. An entire odyssey can be organised within a few days, thanks to Google, TripAdvisor and email. It is more than the logistics that have changed, though. The communication revolution of the last quarter century has influenced travel culture and has profoundly impacted my life.

I had completed my first university degree before I saw my first email. Mark, a hip young Latin lecturer who brought a 'dead' language to life, showed me how he could send a letter to his sister in the United States and receive a reply within minutes. I embraced online communication in all its 1990s forms, used rudimentary HTML to mock up a primitive website and spent every hour I could afford in Yahoo's online chat program (we didn't call them apps in the twentieth century). Despite frequent disconnections and the cacophonous babble of my modem straining to shake hands with the World Wide Web, I made firm friends with the regulars in our Trivia chatroom. I fell in love with one of them long before online dating became A Thing, leading to my move from South Africa to Chile, and I went on to meet others in my travels around the world. It was some of these friends – including two we sadly lost to disease in the 2020s – who discussed olives, alphabets and toilet paper while I was in Monemvasia.

I sometimes wonder: were it not for that initial big move, how would it all have turned out?

Now we have Facebook, WhatsApp, Instagram, Twitter and numerous other platforms onto which I have not yet ventured. A traveller never has to feel alone, not unless that's what they want. In Sri Lanka, my exploration of the country was a solitary undertaking. Ten years later, in Greece, the vibrancy of my friends' messages enhanced my adventures. They shared my excitements and frustrations every step of the way.

My social media posts served as a valuable resource when recalling the emotion of each discovery. At the beginning, I used them purely for reference. Soon, I was slotting snippets of posts into the story to break up the narrative and to let readers hear my immediate, raw impressions come through the more crafted text. Using Facebook extracts as a literary device has been interesting: some beta readers loved them and asked for more, others loathed them. I kept the posts authentic, doing no more than tweaking them here or there – trimming superfluous detail, correcting a typo, or inserting a phrase to make the context clear.

And I love the mini theme that materialised, and which I hadn't realised was a metaphor until an editor pointed it out:

one woman's journey from olive aversion to olive addiction. Almost as much as I now love olives. But not quite.

By the time I returned to Australia, I had a new comprehension of how good I have it. Jenny had reminded me that, fifteen years prior to posting that photograph of the Lego Acropolis, we had been in Lima. Her comment got me calculating that it had been exactly three years since I'd been in Prague with Shauna. And six months, within a couple of days, since Adam and I had left Delhi. I understand now that the opportunities I've had to travel the world more than compensate for day-to-day mundanity.

I thought that recovering my wanderlust would be what made my life extraordinary, but another secret awaited me. My subconscious knew there was something else I needed, and it told me in the form of a dream. It was writing that would add layers of meaning to my existence – the long learning process of honing the craft, the self-awareness that comes from accepting criticism, the resilience needed to survive punishing rejection, the discipline to sit at the keyboard month after month.

And the breakthroughs about myself and my family. Sometimes, for the sake of the narrative, I've pinned a moment of mindfulness to an event or a geographical place. There *were* epiphanies – confronting my privilege on the lip of Santorini's volcano was the most powerful – but the discoveries emerged not only when I was physically in

Greece, but also in the years I toiled over translating my experiences into words on paper.

~ ~ ~

It took a further five years of growth, as a woman and as a writer, to progress from first draft to final. COVID-19 shattered our world, and I battled to focus on my computer's screen. When Australia's borders clanged shut, keeping us safe but isolated, Megan was the living person I missed the most. I was scared for my family and the country of my birth, with its own hard-to-seal borders and its lack of medical resources. When the ocean that separated us became uncrossable, it brought a scrap of comfort to picture that little Meteora magnet on Megan's fridge in Cape Town.

Just as I had in the aftermath of my Sri Lankan accident, I shrank from the world. I returned to labour in the garden of my manuscript, pruning a chapter here, grafting two passages there. Even as my exterior life diminished, the world in my head – and on the page – flourished.

If ever there was a time to reflect on one's own privilege, that time is now. COVID-19 has made me more conscious of gratitude than I've ever been. For windows that open, and our view of the giant trees on the hill behind the high-rise block of flats across the road. For having more doors that close in our little apartment than people: no matter how much Adam and I love each other, we each need our own space. For the relative security of my job, and that I can do some of it from home. I am thankful for the infrastructure that services our building: How much harder must it be to self-isolate if, as for so many around the globe, you have no internet access, if you have to collect water from a communal tap, if you have to share a toilet with other families? If you need to choose between keeping your loved ones safe from infection or putting that day's food on the table?

How much harder if, as in Greece, your country's economy relies in large part on a robust travel industry?

We said, 'We're all in this together,' and to some extent that was true. But let's not fool ourselves that the effects of this pandemic were equal for everyone, between countries or even within the borders of one country.

~ ~ ~

I'll never know my mother as a person in her own right, rather than as a parent, but at last, two decades after her death, I feel as if I've shared something real with her, one adult woman to another.

She can't see me as I tip my hat to her kindness and her own brand of courage. She can't know my regrets about the times I hurt her, or that I've learned to regard our differences – for the most part – with fond respect. I wish I had some sense of belonging with her. I've found a measure of peace, though, albeit tinged with the sadness of lost opportunities.

That peace saturated my unexpected second journey to Greece, turning it into a far gentler odyssey than the first – but that's another story.

# EPILOGUE
## A QUEST AND A COVER

IN MAY 2022, MY siblings were packing up my brother's house when they found an envelope. Inside was a treasure: a snapshot of my mother and grandmother sitting on the steps of a Greek temple.

The photograph wasn't great. It was badly faded and discoloured. And the composition was terrible. In the upper left, perched against three – no, make that four – columns, the women only just managed to stay in shot. Their outfits were familiar from my childhood but odd from the perspective of twenty-first-century travel: my mum had a large handbag on her lap, and I just *knew* my gran was wearing pantyhose. The columns seemed to lean over on the drunken cusp of collapse, but that was because the whole picture was off kilter, shot with a skewed lens. The foreground was dominated by the fractured stone steps taking up at least half the frame.

The image didn't appear to have a single useful feature to identify its location. Mum's 1978 diary narrowed the setting down to somewhere in Athens or on Aegina, Poros or Hydra, the three Saronic islands she visited on a day trip from Piraeus. Anyone who's had the good fortune of travelling in Greece, though, would know that covered a lot of possibilities.

A monochrome filter cleaned the pic up a bit. On a whim, I posted it on Instagram, Twitter and Facebook as an inverted #MidMonthMapMystery, one I was sure would never be solved.

The comments poured in. A few guesses, some chat about how conservation awareness has changed access to heritage sites over the decades, a couple of observations on family resemblances, a lot of appreciation for the value of the find. Bob, an American friend I met in our 1990s chatroom, had a go at lightening the image so we could better see my mum's face.

Then Mohammed, a friend since our Abu Dhabi teaching days, tagged *his* friend, Karl in Beirut, and the game changed. Karl Azzam has a PhD in archaeology, and in his eyes the structure was anything but nondescript.

The first thing he noticed was that some of the columns were closer together than others, and some were bulkier than the rest. He reminded me of the optical illusion Dimitri had pointed out on my first day in Athens, but which I wouldn't have had a clue how to spot for myself. Ancient architects used variations in spacing and girth to play with perspective. Together with subtle angles and curves, these made the Parthenon, perched atop the hill of the Acropolis, look perfectly rectilinear from the streets below.

Then came the kicker. 'Plus there are breaks at the bottom of the last two columns that match with the main façade on the doorway side.' The recent photograph Karl added to his comment showed the very same cracks visible in my family snapshot.

To say I was overwhelmed – both with gratitude and with a renewed awareness of how the internet brings together people from many lands – would be an understatement. As my Chilean friend Valeria commented, 'This whole conversation is amazing! Social media put to its best use.' It's hard to be a hundred percent certain of anything, but I have a high degree of confidence that Karl pinpointed the exact location where my mother and grandmother sat in 1978.

But that's not the end of the story.

I was on such a high from this exchange that I wrote an account for my author newsletter. And then the episode was closed, and I shifted the warm inner glow of this discovery to the back burner.

Until two days later. When the first proofs of *Unpacking for Greece*'s front cover landed in my inbox.

You see, my cover designer doesn't get my newsletters, and he doesn't follow me on social media. He hasn't even read *Unpacking for Greece*, because that's not how cover designers work. What he had was a detailed brief, including a summary of the book. I'd requested an eye-catching image with a contemporary feel, but I had also asked if my mother could be represented, possibly with some element extracted from her photograph or diary. This would be a tribute to my mum and a symbol of the unexpected way Greece had brought her back to me.

It would also signal the book's genre to prospective readers. Getting a book into the wrong hands doesn't serve anyone well. The last thing I wanted was to attract readers who might be put off by the more personal aspects of my journey.

Two concept proofs arrived. One was completely unsuitable. The other blew me away. Without knowing anything about my search for the photo's location, Andrew had captured its essence.

There was a small niggle that the image might be misleading. To clear up any misunderstanding:

> 1. The title font isn't my mother's handwriting, and that's not my hand, either.
> 2. The photograph didn't accompany me to Greece. I didn't even know it existed until a few months before publication.
> 3. The temple on the cover *is* the Parthenon – not too surprising, given that it is Greece's most famous building – but that isn't the spot where my mum and gran posed for the snapshot.

The cover isn't 'real'. But it's a metaphor, of sorts, for the spirit of my Greek travels. For how they became a quest to turn a page in my life, and for how my mum's tiny journal turned out to be an unexpected travel companion.

# WHAT HAPPENED NEXT

Just how did growing up in apartheid South Africa lead to Sally's unexpected second Greek trip, decades later? Read on for a free preview of her next book, *Packing for Greece: A Gentler Odyssey*, which takes the reader to eleven destinations across the Greek mainland and islands.

## But first…

Sign up to *Journeys in Pages*, Sally's free email newsletter for readers, travellers and writers. Subscribers receive a bonus: the full story of what happened to Sally and her sisters in Peru.

**www.eepurl.com/hewm69**

Enjoyed this book?
Please leave a review wherever you bought it —
even one short sentence makes more of a difference
than you might think.

Want to see or hear more?
Visit **www.linktr.ee/SallyJaneSmith** for
heaps of Greek-themed treats, including gorgeous
photos, podcasts and travel games.

Interested in helping an author out?
Ask your local library to stock *Unpacking for Greece.*

Looking for a community of like-minded readers
and writers who love memoirs in general and travel
narratives in particular?
Join the friendliest group on Facebook,
*We Love Memoirs.*

# BOOK TWO: CHAPTER ONE
# REMEMBERING APARTHEID
# SOUTH AFRICA

I'D BEEN PLANNING THE Canadian visit for months.

Five days before my scheduled flight, my passport and air ticket sat ready on a table in my Australian flat. A suitcase lay open in a corner of the room, half filled with a jumble of travel essentials. I'd even invested in a couple of luxuries: a power bank and an extra memory card for my phone. There'd be no chance of a low battery or lack of space forcing me to choose between photos of landmarks or candid family snapshots. I was all set to explore Vancouver during the last week of a mild May, before heading up to the Rocky Mountains with my nephew, Christopher.

So how did I end up disembarking at Athens International Airport instead, a mere eight months after my life-changing first journey to Greece?

To understand the bizarre twist that threw my plans

into disarray, we'll need to go back in time. A long way back, to the dying days of apartheid.

~ ~ ~

My parents were kind people who tried to lead good lives. They attended a church that was about as non-racial a place of worship as existed in South Africa at the time, and sought out schools for us that admitted pupils of all races. They made real sacrifices to help people in need, and raised us to make friends and respect our elders regardless of skin colour.

But make no mistake, I grew up complicit in – and benefitting from – the institutions of racial oppression.

Imagine, if you will, two teenagers on the half-hour afternoon walk from school to the train station. She's fair-haired and self-conscious about her inability to catch a tan. He's what is termed 'Cape Coloured' in apartheid's endless obsession with racial sub-classifications. They've been classmates for years and get on well: they banter together during lessons, go to many of the same after-school activities, dance at weekend parties. They both score high marks, just one rung down from the three acknowledged brainiacs in their year. They're not especially close, but she considers him a friend.

Mid-chat, she parrots a gag from a poorly photocopied sheet that's been handed around school in the way these things were done before the internet gave us memes. It's a weak joke that relies on racial degradation for its humour, but she hasn't given this a thought. She's suppressing a giggle, waiting for his explosive laugh at the punchline.

Instead – to her shock, because she's had the privilege of ignoring the systemic imbalance of power that lurks beneath their friendship – he calls her out.

It's less shameful to pretend that girl wasn't me, but I'm not fooling anybody.

Powerful as this memory is, I have no recollection of my friend's words. But the takeaway message was clear: *It's easy to claim skin colour doesn't matter, if you're not the one bleeding because of it.*

Once he'd confronted me with the relentless violations of apartheid, it was impossible to let things go. The blinkers were off and, everywhere I turned, I witnessed the brutal underbelly of my soft lifestyle. Before I left high school, I became a political activist.

Let's put that statement in perspective. Yes, there were white heroes in the struggle against racial injustice, both sung and unsung, and I am honoured to know a few. But they were not many, and I was not one of them.

Nevertheless, although my role in the uprising was so minor as to fade into insignificance, it was all-consuming for me. At seventeen, I joined a Cape Youth Congress branch that gathered in the crypt of an Anglican church on Sunday evenings.

My mother agreed to ferry me into the city every Sunday. With the lack of mindfulness typical of an adolescent, it didn't occur to me what a bother it was for her to drive the forty-kilometre round trip. With hindsight, I suspect that my parents, who were grappling with my decision to leave their faith, hoped the church connection was much more than a convenient venue. But CAYCO wasn't a religious organisation. It acted as a wing of the African National Congress Youth League, which had gone into exile when the government banned the ANC in 1960.

Mum continued to schlep me to and fro every week until I finished school, got a full-time job in a city bank and, unable to afford a place of my own, moved into Cape Town's YWCA. This communal residence for young women gave me an independence from my family I considered well worth the evening curfews and weekly mandatory religious services. Its location within walking distance of the CAYCO meetings was a valuable bonus.

~ ~ ~

Nelson Mandela's release from prison on 11 February 1990 marked my political coming of age.

Years before emails were commonplace, the summons came through the activist phone network. The YWCA's payphone was tucked behind a staircase, in an uncomfortable nook usually filled with giggling gossip or murmured endearments. This call was to be very different. It was a Saturday, just a few hours before the public announcement that Mandela would walk free the next afternoon, and the voice on the other end of the line was flustered. The caller was working their way through a lengthy phone list, mobilising community activists to help with preparations for a rally to welcome him.

Rumour and conjecture had been running wild for the last eight days. On 2 February, headlines had blazoned out the news of the unbanning of Mandela's African National Congress and other organisations that had campaigned against apartheid for decades. Since then, almost every conversation turned to whether the government would release its most famous political prisoner, and when. This hurried exchange on the YWCA payphone wasn't speculation, though. This time it was real. I signed out of the building for the night, as we would be hard at work until long after my curfew.

Hundreds converged on the University of the Western Cape, *toyi-toying* in a joyous frenzy of celebration while we waited for our leaders to assign tasks. Many of us were oblivious to the logistical monster they were tackling behind the scenes. While we chanted and danced, they were struggling to confirm a venue for the largest gathering Cape Town had ever seen.

We split into groups, each with a job to do. My team's brief was to replicate a hastily designed pamphlet with a simple message in black on white: 'Mandela speaks Parade Sun 11 Feb 3pm'. I piled paper into a wheezy old photocopier. My friends tackled the results, some with scissors, others using rulers to tear the sheets into careful halves. 'How can we have a revolution,' we joked, 'if we don't have a guillotine?'

Early on Sunday morning, a bunch of CAYCO youth piled into an old VW Kombi minibus draped with the ANC flag. This blatant display was an act of both pride and insurrection; it wasn't long since it had been an imprisonable offence. Fuelled by adrenaline and a couple of hours' sleep, we drove through seaside suburbs, calling out the news until we were hoarse. Our aim was to let all who wanted to welcome this great man – especially Black domestic workers living in the 'servants' quarters' of white households – know they could come to the Parade to hear him speak.

The Grand Parade was once Cape Town's main public square, but in 1990 it was just a paved space in front of the historic City Hall building that had been repurposed to house a cramped library and a few municipal services. The square itself was underused, except for the busy kiosks selling takeaway food along one edge.

On that day, the Grand Parade was unrecognisable. My heart soared at the sight of the ANC's green, black and gold colours flying from the City Hall, and the thousands upon thousands of people streaming in from every direction, more than I have ever seen in one place, before or since. But as the hot hours wore on with no sign of Mandela, the crowd grew larger. Thirstier. Angrier.

A confusion of human figures covered every surface, clambering up to every vantage point. The roofs of the kiosks lining the edge of the Grand Parade collapsed from the burden of the bodies they bore, as did the tower that had been set up for the press. People swarmed up tall palm trees and thudded to the ground when sturdy fronds snapped under their weight. I later heard that former United States presidential candidate Jesse Jackson had insisted, against the advice of rally organisers, on riding 'through the people'. Marshals had to pass him and his wife over the heads of the throng and drag them up to the speakers' balcony. The load of those climbing onto the roof of their abandoned car flattened it.

A hand grasped my shoulder. It belonged to a man who pulled me into a line of marshals and then vanished into the mêlée. Perhaps he chose me for the struggle slogan on my T-shirt. Maybe he simply grabbed whoever was closest. But I was eighteen years old, just three months out of high school and politically aware for not much longer. I had never been a rally marshal and had only a simplistic understanding of what was happening. All I knew was what he hollered into my ear, barely heard above the surrounding din and clamour. People were being crushed at the front, and lives depended on us damming the swelling flood of those desperate to get close to Mandela, to see his face for the first time.

Arms linked with strangers, the fragile chain of marshals staggered under the surging force of the hundred-thousand-strong crowd. We broke apart, then fought to come together, stretching urgent hands out to each other until we could again feel the precarious grip of sweat-slick fingers.

Spittle from angry mouths, scant inches away, flecked my face.

'Where were you at Sharpeville?' The man's voice cracked, mid-yell, on the name of the town where police killed or wounded more than 250 Black South Africans during the 1960 massacre.

'Where were you in '76?' shouted someone else I couldn't see.

They had a point. What right did this little whitey, an incongruous patch in the line of marshals, have to stand in their way on this day of all days? It's not lost on me now that, whatever the circumstances, I was yet another white person telling people of colour what they could or could not do.

Gunfire rang out as gangsters looted nearby shops. I had to choke down my panic. *Are police firing into the crowd?* It had happened before and would again. Without handheld radios or mobile phones, we had no way to find out. All we could do was the job in front of us: hold our thin human line against the shoving ocean of people as best we could.

There was relief when the multitude thinned after the ordeal of so many hours, but there was also a cloud of dismay settling on the thousands still there. We had just about given up hope of hearing Tata Mandela speak. I was sitting on the ground in a sun-struck daze, with my head in my hands, when there was a roar of euphoria. The drifting currents of the crowd poured back into the vortex. Mandela had arrived at last. The distinctive timbre of his voice flowed over us as the summer sky dissolved into darkness.

It was both the most wonderful and the most dreadful day of my young life.

The ray of memory refracts through a prism, separating the momentous from the mundane. As if it were yesterday, I feel the impact of that first glimpse of his face. How different he looked from the twenty-seven-year-old photographs, which were all most of us had ever seen of him. Then the prism shifts, the light bends, and I can taste the nausea of the heat exhaustion that laid me low for days afterwards, probe the stinging blister that festered on my sunburnt lip.

I have had many privileges, and one of them was hearing the rising tide of Tata Mandela's voice washing over his tired people, weary from hours of waiting, weary from centuries of waiting. Within two minutes, he'd made a commitment to the South African nation to 'place the remaining years of my life in your hands'. This was a pledge behind which he stood until his death at the age of ninety-five. His final months were hard. I'm glad he is at rest now, after a lifetime of service to his country. His party may have disappointed many of us in the decades following his presidency, but he never did.

~ ~ ~

In the months that followed, while I never suffered anything close to the same hardships and dangers faced by my Black comrades, I did learn what it was to be afraid.

The bitter huddle over burning newspaper as we gasped through clouds of teargas.

The favourite T-shirt I pulled from my pack to bind the leg of a stranger, injured in a police baton charge. Her limb had been gashed through layers of skin and fat and muscle, and I woke from graphic nightmares of that wounded flesh for months.

The panic of falling, myself, in the stampede away from that same charge. My boyfriend hauled me from under hundreds of trampling feet but, like a Cinderella who'd danced at a particularly unenjoyable ball, all I lost was a single shoe.

~ ~ ~

Curious about this decades-old history
and how it led to Sally's second trip to Greece?

Want to keep exploring the
Greek mainland and islands?

Sign up to Sally Jane Smith's newsletter at
**www.eepurl.com/hewm69**
to be notified when the next instalment in the
*Packing for Greece* series lands on shelves,
or visit
**www.linktr.ee/SallyJaneSmith**
to access gorgeous photos, travel puzzles,
podcasts and more.

# ACKNOWLEDGEMENTS

**T**HIS STORY STARTED ITS life as part of a much longer manuscript titled *Just One Step*, which with time and editing became the first two instalments in the *Packing for Greece* series. Much of this work was done on Darkinjung and Guringai land on the NSW Central Coast of Australia. I acknowledge the traditional custodians of this land, and pay my respects to elders past, present and emerging.

It's a terrible thing to rely on clichés, but I'm going to say it: it took a village to raise this book. In the literal sense, this could be the village of Agios Georgios and the writers' retreat named Limnisa on its outskirts. Metaphorically, it is the village of readers, writers and friends, both online and off, who have supported me as my story has grown.

Limnisa wasn't the only writing community to nurture this project. There were the accomplished authors and staff who shared my residency at Varuna, the Writers' House in 2018, and were kind about my naive conviction that my draft was close to final. Charlotte Clutterbuck was especially generous, giving me one-on-one feedback on an excerpt and inviting me to join a regular writers' group we tentatively named Catalyst.

And then, among the many who have shared their experience, there has been the wonderful family of authors associated with the *We Love Memoirs* group on Facebook. They gave me my first opportunity to see my words between book covers, advised on countless technical matters, and cheered me on when I felt overwhelmed. If I start listing names, I'm going to miss someone out. You know who you are.

I'll try not to repeat myself, for fear of these acknowledgements turning out to be longer than the story, but if you're named in this book, you have enriched my travels, my writing or my life.

Between 2016 and 2023, dozens of people critiqued drafts or excerpts. There were alpha readers, beta readers, professional manuscript assessors and editors. Some checked the technical details of a short passage or the spelling of a few Greek words, while others read the full narrative of both books more than once. Some warmed to my story, others not so much. Every single one of them brought something to my writing practice, and I thank them all: Alan Skilbeck, Alyson Sheldrake, Carol Major, Carolyn V. Hamilton, Chris Smith, the writers in Allison Lane's Compassionate Critique sessions, Daniel Stitt-Hatton, Danny Sag, David Hendricks,

## ACKNOWLEDGEMENTS

Dimitra Matsouka, Elisabeth Chretien (and Dan Alexandar, also from NY Book Editors, who referred me to Elisabeth), Emma Skinner, Fanoula Kopsida, Fotini Arbounioti, Ilona Bartsch, Jacqui Brown, Janet Bateman, Jean Gochros, Jenny Gardner, Joshua White, Judith Benson, Katie Butler, Kim Miller, Linda Moren Abuelghanam, Lisa Rose Wright, the anonymous readers from the Queensland Writers Centre Publishable program, Rebecca Stewart, Rhonda Read, Richard Bramley, Shauna Bradley, Simon Michael Prior, Sue Bavey, Susan Soranno, Tania Jadresic, Tassin Barnard, Tony Reeder and Veronica Moore. Any errors or clumsy phrases that made it into the final version are entirely mine. Kate Sclavos, Laura Maya, Valerie Poore and editor Emily Miller, together with my ever-faithful band of 'sisters' and a nephew who has always gone beyond the call, helped me over the finish line.

And thank you to Chris Christensen of the Amateur Traveler podcast and blog, who gave me my first chance to chat about Greece on air and gifted me a tagline – when I felt just about wrung dry of words – for my front cover.

There is a lot more to book production than wordcraft. I am grateful to Andrew and Rebecca Brown from Design for Writers for their perceptive cover design and careful page formatting, to my talented friend Liana Magrath for designing the Journeys in Pages logo, to Karl Schaffarczyk for rescuing me from my Domain Name System blues, and to

Megan McEvoy for holding onto my back-up files and always having my back. Allison K Williams and Ashleigh Renard of The Writers Bridge, indie author Emma Lombard and the Binders online forums have all been unstinting in their writerly guidance. Tina Hartas and Sulari Gentill found the time to read a novice writer's manuscript, and followed up with endorsements that encouraged me in moments of self-doubt. And the Words on the Waves Writers Festival has brought an annual literary celebration to our hometown and created opportunities for local authors.

I am sure there will be others who jump in to assist, in the months after these pages go to print, and I'm equally sure I'll wish it weren't too late to add their names to this list. In fact, there are more people who have supported my writing endeavours than I could possibly name, but please know that I appreciate every one of you.

To my family, friends and colleagues who support my creative work: thank you. You don't know how rare that is in the writing world. And as for the 'Word Warriors' among my Facebook friends, you've made untangling regional English variations a lot more fun than it would otherwise have been.

To Mom. I'm sorry it wasn't easier. You did your best — and so did I, in my own clumsy way. I wish we'd had more time. I hope you don't mind too much that I turned you into 'Mum' for the sake of grammatical consistency.

## ACKNOWLEDGEMENTS

To Aruna Rajapaksa, Chamila and your families. I told the story of the bus accident in *Unpacking for Greece*. In Book Two, I'll share what came next. I will never forget how you helped me.

And to Adam. I can't believe it's been fifteen years since we took that first walk about Walkabout Park. You do so much for me, not least putting up with me when I go into full writing recluse mode or succumb to a sudden need to disappear for weeks on a solo expedition. I'm very lucky to have found you.

Lastly, thank you to every librarian, bookseller and reader who has taken a chance on *Unpacking for Greece*.